Implementing the Every Child Matters Strategy

Implementing the Every Child Matters Strategy is a comprehensive resource for senior leaders, managers of Every Child Matters (ECM) and teachers responsible for leading the government's ECM strategy in primary and secondary schools and other education settings such as academies, sixth form colleges, short stay schools, children's centres and early years settings.

Featuring step-by-step advice, photocopiable checklists and templates, with suggestions for further activities in relation to implementing and embedding the government's ECM strategy in schools/education settings, this practical guide will enable readers to:

- understand the concept and principles of ECM and translate those into developing an ECM policy for their school/setting;
- know their role in moving ECM policy, practice and provision forward;
- understand the importance of ECM well-being for effective learning;
- embed ECM through school improvement planning, target setting, tracking pupils' well-being outcomes and efficient resource deployment;
- identify effective strategies to promote productive partnership working to improve ECM outcomes for children and young people;
- understand the OFSTED inspection requirements for pupils' ECM well-being.

An invaluable resource for those professionals strategically leading ECM in their own education setting, it offers practical guidance, recommended management approaches, models of good practice and signposting to further sources of information on how best to ensure ECM is woven and embedded throughout the school/setting.

Supporting materials are downloadable from: www.routledgeteachers.com/resources/fulton.

Rita Cheminais is an independent consultant for Every Child Matters. She has written a number of valuable books in the area. These include *Every Child Matters: a new role for SENCOs*, *Every Child Matters: a practical guide for teachers* and *Every Child Matters: a practical guide for teaching assistants*. She is contactable on admin@ecm-solutions.org.uk and www.ecm-solutions.org.uk.

Implementing the Every Child Matters Strategy

The essential guide for school leaders and managers

RITA CHEMINAIS

Routledge
Taylor & Francis Group

LONDON AND NEW YORK

First published 2010
by Routledge
2 Park Square, Milton Park, Abingdon, Oxon, OX14 4RN

Simultaneously published in the USA and Canada
by Routledge
270 Madison Avenue, New York, NY 10016

Routledge is an imprint of the Taylor & Francis Group, an informa business

© 2010 Rita Cheminais

Typeset in Garamond and Helvetica by Wearset Ltd, Boldon, Tyne and Wear
Printed and bound in Great Britain by the MPG Books Group

British Library Cataloguing in Publication Data
A catalogue record for this book is available from the British Library

Library of Congress Cataloging-in-Publication Data
Cheminais, Rita.
Implementing the every child matters strategy : the essential guide for school leaders and managers / Rita Cheminais.
p. cm.
Includes bibliographical references and index.
1. Educational evaluation–Great Britain–Handbooks, manuals, etc. 2. Education–Standards–Great Britain–Handbooks, manuals, etc. 3. Education and state–Great Britain–Handbooks, manuals, etc. I. Title.
LB2822.75.C469 2010
379.1´580941–dc22   2009027731

ISBN10: 0-415-49824-4 (pbk)
ISBN10: 0-203-86160-4 (ebk)

ISBN13: 978-0-415-49824-1 (pbk)
ISBN13: 978-0-203-86160-8 (ebk)

Rita Cheminais clearly understands the issues that school leaders and Every Child Matters (ECM) managers need to grapple with to ensure that their schools are developing and sustaining sustainable ECM strategies. In this book she outlines the key features of an ECM strategy, and provides the resources required to help schools implement such a strategy, taking account of 'where they are now' and 'where they want to be'. Readers of the book will be reassured to know that it is up-to-date with regard to relevant national policy developments and carefully linked to the Ofsted's most recent inspection requirements.

Perhaps most importantly, the book is both comprehensive and accessible, and as such is likely to be an essential resource for school leaders, ECM managers, inclusion leaders, SENCOs and other key personnel involved in implementing ECM in their schools and in collaboration with community partners.

Finally, it lends itself to use as an overall guide to developing and implementing an ECM strategy, but it can also be used as a 'toolkit' that leaders and managers can refer to when they need a specific resource.

I can thoroughly recommend the book as an essential 'one stop' guide to ECM policy and practice in schools.

Christopher Robertson
Lecturer in Inclusive Education, University of Birmingham and Editor of the SENCO Update

Contents

List of Figures and Tables

Acknowledgements

I wish to thank all the leaders and senior managers in schools and local authorities who I have met on my travels across England and Wales, who identified the urgent need for a practical book – like this essential guide – to enable them to successfully implement and embed the government's Every Child Matters strategy.

I am grateful to NASEN colleagues and those in higher education institutions who continue to promote and refer to my publications on Every Child Matters. I have appreciated the words of wisdom from Philip Eastwood, the Advanced Skills Teacher for Initial Teacher Training at St Mary's and St Paul's CE Primary School in Knowsley, who reassures me that a practical book of this nature will be welcomed by school leaders and managers who have raised standards and who are now ready to switch their focus to the Every Child Matters agenda.

I wish to thank my editors, Dr Monika Lee and Annamarie Kino at Routledge Education, for supporting my proposal for a book of this nature. I am also grateful to Sophie Thomson, Editorial Assistant, for her support during the production of this book.

My final thanks go to the following organisations for allowing the reproduction of materials with kind permission:

- Department for Children, Schools and Families
- National Foundation for Educational Research
- Qualifications and Curriculum Authority
- Training and Development Agency for Schools.

Abbreviations

ALS	additional literacy support
CAF	common assessment framework
CPD	continuing professional development
CRB	Criminal Records Bureau
CWDC	Children's Workforce Development Council
DCSF	Department for Children, Schools and Families
DH	Department of Health
DSG	Dedicated Schools Grant
EAL	English as an Additional Language
ECM	Every Child Matters
ELS	early literacy support
ES	extended services
FE	further education
FLS	further literacy support
FMSiS	Financial Management Standards in Schools
FSM	free school meals
GSCC	General Social Care Council
GTC	General Teaching Council for England
HE	higher education
HLTA	higher level teaching assistant
ICT	information and communication technology
INSET	in-service education and training
ITT	initial teacher training
KS	key stage
LA	local authority
LAC	looked after children
LDD	learning difficulties and/or disabilities
NASEN	National Association of Special Educational Needs
NCLSCS	National College for Leadership of Schools and Children's Services
NCSL	National College for School Leadership
NMC	Nursing and Midwifery Council
NSF	National Service Framework
OFSTED	Office for Standards in Education, Children's Services and Skills
PA	personal adviser
PASS	Pupil Attitudes to Self and School
PE	physical education
PRU	pupil referral unit (also known as a 'short stay school' in England)
PSHE	personal, social and health education

PSHCE	personal, social, health and citizenship education
QCA	Qualifications and Curriculum Authority
QCDA	Qualifications and Curriculum Development Agency
RAG	red, amber, green (rating system)
RE	religious education
SDP	school development plan
SEAL	social and emotional aspects of learning
SEF	self-evaluation form
SEN	special educational needs
SENCO	special educational needs coordinator
SIP	School Improvement Partner
SMSC	spiritual, moral, social and cultural
SRE	sex and relationships education
TA	teaching assistant
TAC	team around the child
TDA	Training and Development Agency for Schools
TES	*Times Educational Supplement*
TLR	teaching and learning responsibility
UPS	upper pay spine

The Aim of this Book

The aim of this book is to enable all those leaders and managers of Every Child Matters (ECM) in early years settings, schools, academies and short stay schools to:

- understand the concept, legal requirements and the latest developments in ECM, and translate those into policy and practice;
- know their strategic role in implementing and embedding ECM across the school;
- understand the link between personalised learning and ECM;
- know how to deploy resources for ECM effectively;
- know how to foster productive collaborative partnerships in order to secure better ECM outcomes for children and young people;
- be familiar with the latest OFSTED inspection requirements in relation to ECM and pupil well-being;
- know where to find further information and resources on ECM.

Who is the book for?

The book is useful to:

- all school leaders, heads of children's centres, academies and short stay schools;
- special educational needs coordinators, inclusion coordinators, leaders of pupil well-being
- local authority ECM managers, advisers, consultants and educational psychologists;
- senior lecturers in higher education and at the National College for Leadership of Schools and Children's Services who are delivering courses on ECM to school leaders and senior managers;
- School Improvement Partners;
- Office for Standards in Education, Children's Services and Skills inspectors.

How the book is designed to be used

This book provides a valuable resource that can:

- provide a quick point of reference for busy professionals leading ECM in a range of educational settings;
- inform ECM policy and practice;
- support the professional development of senior management within the purchasing institution, by providing photocopiable and downloadable materials.

Supporting materials can be downloaded from: www.routledgeteachers.com/resources/fulton.

Introduction

The government, in their Green Paper published in September 2003, introduced and outlined their ambitious plans for transforming services for all children and young people, and in particular the vulnerable or those at risk of poor outcomes, in order to protect, nurture and improve their life chances and well-being outcomes in relation to them being healthy, staying safe, enjoying and achieving, making a positive contribution, and achieving economic well-being.

Through the Children Act 2004, the Every Child Matters Change for Children Programme, the government's Children's Plan, the Every Child Matters (ECM) outcomes framework, and the National Service Framework (NSF) for Children, Young People and Maternity Services, all of which make up the ECM strategy, schools as universal service providers, along with health, social care and youth justice, are expected to work collaboratively in order to intervene early before things go wrong in children's lives.

The school's contribution to improving children and young people's well-being was strengthened further through the development of: extended services in or near the school site; a renewed Office for Standards in Education, Children's Services and Skills (OFSTED) inspection framework and self evaluation form (SEF) centred around the ECM outcomes; greater integrated working across agencies; the introduction of children's centres; and the common core of skills and knowledge for the wider children's workforce.

The Education and Inspections Act 2006, Section 38(1), effective from September 2007, placed a new duty on the governing body of primary, secondary and special maintained schools, pupil referral units (PRUs) (now short stay schools) and academies, to promote the well-being of pupils in terms of the five ECM outcomes that go to make a good life:

* their physical and mental health and emotional well-being;
* protection from harm and neglect;
* education, training and recreation;
* the contribution made by them to society; and
* their social and economic well-being.

The notion that well-being promotes educational attainment and supports the whole child is reflected in the government's thinking that ECM and standards go hand-in-hand, complementing each other, and being realised through personalisation: no standards without ECM and no ECM without standards has become the government's mantra.

The links between good emotional and physical well-being and the readiness and engagement of a child or young person to learn and develop good behaviour and academic achievement are crucial. Knowing each child or young person and how his or her family circumstances impact on their ECM well-being outcomes is important. Government initiatives such as extended schools, Healthy Schools Status, the social and emotional aspects of learning (SEAL) programme, and the Early

Years and Foundation Stage curriculum have all helped to address the balance between children and young people's physical, social and emotional development with their cognitive development.

The government, in their publication *21st Century Schools: A World-Class Education for Every Child* (DCSF 2008b), identified that schools working with other services – such as health and social care – and focused on delivering the five ECM outcomes is an essential way of raising standards. They considered that twenty-first-century schools:

> play a central role in improving the aspects of a child's life – physical health, emotional well-being, safety, opportunity for wider experiences and the development of skills – that characterise a good and enjoyable childhood and set up a young person for success as an adult.
>
> (DCSF 2008: 13)

The government expects the twenty-first-century school, in relation to ECM and pupil well-being, to:

- address the needs of the whole child or young person through a personalised and tailored approach in relation to teaching and learning and their personal and social development;
- provide every child or young person with a key adult (personal tutor) who knows them well, guides and monitors their progress, and responds quickly if any problems arise;
- ensure school staff, and not just teachers, identify children and young people's additional needs accurately and early, and provide access to the extra support required to meet those needs;
- engage and consult pupils about learning, well-being and other issues relating to aspects of school life in general;
- engage parents and carers in their child's learning and development, providing access to support to enable them to do this more effectively;
- place a greater importance and emphasis on working in partnership with other schools, early years providers, colleges, higher education (HE) institutions, children's services and Children's Trusts to safeguard and improve children and young people's lives and well-being;
- take responsibility for improving other children and young people's outcomes in the wider community, in addition to those enrolled in their own setting.

A school's contribution to partnership working and pupil well-being is reflected in the renewed OFSTED inspection framework, effective from September 2009. This new inspection schedule incorporates the school-level pupil well-being indicators, which are designed to recognise a school's progress in helping to improve children and young people's lives. The government guidance on pupil well-being, published in 2009, also emphasised the importance of schools' contributions in promoting pupils' well-being.

The new School Report Card to be introduced by the government in 2011, which will replace the School Profile, will contain information and data about achievements relating to pupils' well-being in the performance category entitled 'Wider Outcomes'. It is envisaged that the School Improvement Partner (SIP) and OFSTED will use the School Report Card, alongside the school's self-evaluation, to identify and discuss areas of strength and development with the headteacher in relation to pupils' well-being, which will subsequently inform the school improvement steps required next in this aspect.

ECM offers those leading and managing the implementation of the ECM strategy in schools and other child-centred settings opportunities and challenges, particularly in relation to partnership working with others to promote and improve pupils' well-being outcomes and to remove barriers to learning.

The implications of ECM for leaders and managers in schools

The ECM manager, as the change agent and ambassador for ECM in a school will need to:

- develop a whole-school vision, policy and ethos for ECM;
- support the continuing professional development (CPD) of the school's children's workforce in ECM in order to build greater capacity;
- advise staff on how to embed ECM across the curriculum and adopt a personalised approach to pupil well-being;
- raise the profile of ECM and pupil well-being within the school and in the wider community;
- challenge any under-achievement and low expectations in relation to the ECM well-being outcomes;
- facilitate innovative practice and look for opportunities to promote ECM;
- promote a solution-focused approach to problem-solving among staff and external partners in relation to ECM;
- gather robust evidence to evaluate and demonstrate the impact of additional provision, interventions and initiatives on improving pupils' ECM well-being outcomes;
- disseminate good practice in ECM with other schools.

Each chapter in this essential guide offers leaders and managers of ECM practical guidance, advice and approaches for embedding this national agenda successfully at the heart of everything the school does.

Chapter 1 focuses on the strategic direction and development of ECM and what this entails for ECM managers in schools in relation to policy, budget planning, provision management and improvement planning.

Chapter 2 covers: the role of the ECM manager; building, leading and managing a school ECM team; and how to make best use of national ECM planning tools and frameworks.

Chapter 3 explores: the links between ECM and personalised learning; how to embed ECM across the curriculum; how to make best use of the school-level indicators and other information on pupil well-being to inform ECM target setting; how to engage pupils in the review of their own progress in the ECM outcomes; and how to publicise the school's achievements in ECM.

Chapter 4 looks at how to develop effective partnerships with other agencies, schools, parents and carers and the community in strengthening the delivery of provision to improve the five ECM outcomes within a school.

Chapter 5 focuses on meeting the OFSTED inspection requirements for ECM and pupil well-being, and how to evaluate the impact of interventions and initiatives on improving pupils' ECM well-being outcomes.

Every chapter offers further questions for reflection, to enable school leaders and managers of ECM to explore this aspect in greater depth, within their own setting or organisation. As a reflective leader and manager of ECM, it is envisaged that by using this book you will secure better ECM well-being outcomes for the children and young people within your school or setting.

1

Strategic Direction and Development of Every Child Matters

This chapter covers:

- recruiting and appointing a manager for Every Child Matters (ECM);
- the role of the governing body and school staff for ECM;
- developing the ECM vision, policy and charter;
- provision management and mapping for ECM;
- budget allocation for ECM;
- development planning for ECM;
- whole-school target setting for ECM outcomes;
- information for the School Report Card on ECM;
- questions for further reflection.

Recruiting and appointing a manager for ECM

Forward-thinking schools in the twenty-first century, as part of workforce remodelling, are appointing a manager for ECM to oversee this important government strategy. The manager for ECM plays a pivotal role in driving ECM throughout the school. For this important strategic role, it is crucial to appoint the appropriate person who will be an effective change agent and have a positive impact on promoting ECM well-being among all pupils.

The manager of ECM requires the backing and support of the headteacher and the governing body. They are an important member of the senior leadership team and are frequently expected to take on the strategic management of ECM alongside their role as a deputy headteacher or assistant headteacher.

The first step to recruiting a manager of ECM is to produce a concise and clearly worded advertisement that portrays an accurate description of the requirements for this high-profile position, in order to attract the highest calibre of prospective applicants. The example of the advertisement illustrated in Figure 1.1 provides a generic model that can be tailored or customised to suit the context and phase of the education setting. It gives a general overview of the role and attributes required by such a key senior member of staff. The scale of pay will be governed by the group and size of the school. The advertisement should appear in the Times Educational Supplement (TES), in the local newspaper and in the local authority (LA) job bulletin. The advertisement, along with an application form, job description and person specification, should also be made available online by the school, the TES and the LA.

A model job description and person specification for a manager of ECM are illustrated in Figures 1.2 and 1.3, both of which may be tailored and adapted to suit the context and phase of the school or other education setting.

Assistant Headteacher: Manager of Every Child Matters
MPS/UPS + TLR2b

Required for September 2010: an enthusiastic, highly motivated, committed qualified teacher with excellent pastoral experience to lead on all aspects of Every Child Matters in the school.

The core purpose of the role will be to implement and manage the ECM strategy, in order to ensure high standards in the five ECM well-being outcomes for pupils.

The qualities, skills and experience required:

- A secure knowledge of the government's ECM initiative.
- A proven track record of promoting and improving pupils' ECM well-being.
- Excellent communication skills in all formats.
- Proven negotiation, influencing and partnership skills.
- A commitment to enhancing staff professional development for ECM.
- An ability to lead, motivate, inspire and support staff.
- An ability to use and analyse pupil-level ECM outcomes data to support target setting.
- Experience in monitoring and evaluating ECM outcomes.
- High expectations of staff, pupils and partner external agencies.

The school offers:

- Membership on the school's dynamic senior leadership team.
- Bespoke professional development.
- Committed and supportive staff and governors.
- Friendly pupils.
- A pleasant working environment with a dedicated office and laptop computer.
- A non-teaching commitment during the first year of ECM strategy implementation.

An application form and further details about the post are available from and returnable to the school.

Closing date for applications: Midday Wednesday 5th May 2010.
Interviews: Week beginning 17th May 2010.

Figure 1.1 Model advertisement for a manager of ECM

From: *Implementing the Every Child Matters Strategy*, Routledge © Rita Cheminais 2010

Assistant Headteacher: Manager of Every Child Matters MPS/UPS + TLR2b

JOB DESCRIPTION

Responsible to: the headteacher

Responsible for: implementing and managing all aspects of the Every Child Matters strategy within the school.

Principal purpose: to manage a whole-school response to ECM; to provide guidance to staff on best practice in ECM in order to secure improved ECM well-being outcomes for pupils; to liaise closely with the headteacher, the governor responsible for ECM, the Curriculum, Assessment, Partnership and Extended School managers.

Main duties and responsibilities:

1 To develop an agreed whole-school vision, policy and charter for ECM.

2 To embed ECM across the curriculum as part of personalised learning.

3 To develop staff capacity to successfully deliver the ECM outcomes.

4 To monitor and evaluate the whole-school policy, provision and targets for ECM.

5 To produce a development plan for ECM which reflects the school improvement priorities for ECM.

6 To disseminate best practice in ECM within and beyond the school.

7 To manage the budget for ECM, identify new funding opportunities and ensure best value.

8 To keep up-to-date with national developments in ECM.

9 To lead and oversee the school's participation in the national ECM Standards Award.

10 To oversee and coordinate the work of the school's ECM team.

11 To act as a champion for pupils' ECM well-being.

12 To undertake any other duties and responsibilities as may be assigned by the headteacher, which are commensurate with the grade of the job.

The school is committed to safeguarding and promoting the welfare of children and young people. The successful applicant will be required to undertake an Enhanced Disclosure with the CRB.

Figure 1.2 Model job description for a manager of ECM

From: *Implementing the Every Child Matters Strategy*, Routledge © Rita Cheminais 2010

Assistant headteacher/manager of ECM			
Aspect	**Minimum requirements**	**Essential**	**Desirable**
Qualifications	• Qualified Teacher Status • Evidence of further study in ECM • Higher degree in educational management or management in working in a multi-disciplinary context	✓ ✓	 ✓
Experience	• Recent successful pastoral experience in promoting ECM • Partnership working with other colleagues, agencies, parents/carers, the community • Curriculum development in aspects related to well being, e.g. SEAL, PSHE, ECM • Whole-school target setting • Monitoring and evaluating the impact of interventions/initiatives • Managing a team, project initiative or managing change	✓ ✓ ✓	 ✓ ✓ ✓
Skills and abilities	• Ability to contribute to senior leadership team decision-making • Ability to make effective use of ICT • Ability to coach and mentor other staff • Ability to plan and deliver in-service training related to ECM • Ability to problem solve using a solution-focused approach • Ability to manage competing priorities and to deliver results within given timescales • Excellent communication skills	✓ ✓ ✓ ✓ ✓ ✓	 ✓
Knowledge	• A well developed knowledge and understanding of the ECM initiative • A knowledge of the role of Children's Trusts and Children's Services • A knowledge of effective approaches to promote ECM and pupil well-being • A knowledge of the evidence base for quality assuring and evaluating ECM • A knowledge of school improvement planning and self-evaluation process • A knowledge of the principles of best value	✓ ✓ ✓ ✓	 ✓ ✓
Personal qualities	• Creative thinker • Highly motivated • Energetic and well organised • Emphatic and insightful • Decisive and outcomes focused • Sense of humour • Flexible • Reliable and trustworthy	 ✓ ✓ ✓ ✓ ✓ ✓ ✓	✓

Figure 1.3 Model person specification for a manager of ECM

From: *Implementing the Every Child Matters Strategy*, Routledge © Rita Cheminais 2010

Preparing for the interview process

Following the shortlisting process from the application forms received, the headteacher, with members of the governing body, will agree upon the venue, a programme for the interview day, the presentation title, and interview questions. Shortlisted applicants would be expected to arrange a visit to the school prior to the interview day.

Four possible presentation titles are offered in Figure 1.4, along with some suggested interview questions.

The role of the governing body and school staff for ECM

The ECM agenda is a prime consideration for all school governors, who are taking on significant responsibilities to deliver the ECM outcomes. Section 38 (1) of the Education and Inspections Act 2006 states:

> The governing body of a maintained school shall, in discharging their functions relating to the conduct of the school:
>
> • promote the well-being of pupils at the school ...
>
> And that in so doing, the governing body will
>
> • have regard to any relevant Children and Young People's Plan
> • have regard to any views expressed by parents of registered pupils.

The Education and Inspections Act 2006 defined well-being in terms of the five ECM outcomes, and the duty became effective from September 2007. The governing body are responsible for: setting the strategic direction for ECM within the school; ensuring that there is accountability for delivering ECM; and acting as a critical friend on ECM by asking challenging and tough questions. The governing body need to be clear about the school's vision and values for ECM. They need to be well-informed about national and local policies and practice on ECM. The manager of ECM in the school can signpost the governors to relevant documents on the topic, many of which can be found on government websites. However, with over 600 government publications relating to ECM, it may be easier for the manager of ECM in the school to provide helpful summaries of key ECM information from relevant DCSF documents.

A good way of introducing ECM to the governing body is through the use of two Teachers TV videos in the *Governors Matters* series, entitled: *Just for Governors – Ideas from the Box: Every Child Matters*, and *Just for Governors – Ideas from the Box: School Improvement and Well-Being*. Both Teachers TV videos provide a useful resource to open up initial discussions about the types of questions governors should be asking the headteacher and the manager of ECM. These questions include:

• What does ECM look like in our school?
• What are the school's strengths and weaknesses in ECM?
• How well is the school doing in each one of the five ECM outcomes?
• What impact are extended school activities, external agencies and other partnerships having on improving pupils' ECM well-being outcomes?
• How are the ECM outcomes being addressed in the classroom?
• What are the pupils' views about the ECM outcomes in this school?
• How is the school measuring the ECM outcomes?
• What is the correlation between pupils' ECM well-being and pupils' attainment?
• How far do the school's attainment targets link with the five ECM outcomes?

Assistant headteacher/manager of ECM

Examples of presentation titles

One of the presentations would be agreed upon by the interview panel, and this would be given to shortlisted applicants five days before the interview day. Prepare a ten-minute PowerPoint presentation, allowing five additional minutes for questions from the interview panel.

1 The ECM agenda competes and conflicts with the standards agenda. How far do you agree or disagree with this statement?

2 In your role as manager of ECM, how will you enable staff and governors to see the direct link between personalised learning and the ECM outcomes?

3 The DCSF state that schools must ensure the delivery of the five ECM outcomes. In your role as manager of ECM, how will you ensure this occurs in this school?

4 How will you develop an agreed vision for ECM?

Examples of interview questions

1 Can you tell us why you would make an effective manager of ECM?

2 Can you tell us about one successful ECM initiative you have introduced in your current school?

3 How would you develop and build the capacity of the school's workforce to meet the requirements of the government's ECM strategy?

4 Which three ECM priorities would you target first for improvement in this school?

5 After analysing the school's ECM data you notice one class in a year group is achieving poor ECM outcomes. Describe how you would address this issue.

6 What criteria would you use to monitor and evaluate classroom practice in ECM?

7 What practical approaches would you utilise in order to help parents/carers support their child's ECM well-being at home?

8 How would you work with the governing body to keep them up-to-date on the implementation of the ECM strategy and its impact?

9 How would you publicise and disseminate the good practice developed in ECM beyond the school?

11 After your first year in the post, how will you know you have had a positive impact in the implementation of the ECM strategy in the school?

11 Do you have any questions to ask the interview panel?

12 Are you still a firm candidate for the post?

Figure 1.4 Examples of presentations and interview questions

School leaders and the manager of ECM should systematically plan, monitor and evaluate extended school provision against the ECM outcomes and feed back their findings to the governing body in order to further governors' understanding about ECM within the school.

The governing body of the school will look at ECM through the school improvement plan, and they should receive regular updates on the progress being made towards meeting the priorities relating to the ECM outcomes on this plan. While it is important for all governors to have an understanding of ECM and to know what the school's strengths and weaknesses are in relation to this aspect, it is good practice to nominate one governor to be the link governor for ECM, or alternatively to allocate five governors, one to each of the ECM outcomes. This approach helps to embed and thread ECM across the school's governing body.

The role of the link governor for ECM

The role of the governor(s) responsible for ECM or one ECM outcome is to:

- keep abreast of ECM developments nationally, locally and within the school;
- act as a conduit for ECM between the governing body and the school;
- meet with the manager of ECM each term for updates;
- tour the school once per term and visit classrooms to see ECM in practice;
- monitor and review the school budget for ECM to judge best value;
- attend any relevant training or conferences for governors on ECM and disseminate information back to the governing body, headteacher and manager of ECM;
- be involved in the appointment of key school staff for ECM;
- discuss the review of pupil progress in relation to the ECM outcomes;
- act as a champion for children's ECM well-being in the school;
- take a central role in governing body meeting discussions about ECM;
- review the effectiveness of the school's ECM policy annually with the manager of ECM;
- act as a critical friend on ECM;
- be clear about the role of the manager of ECM in school;
- discuss and review the progress being made to meeting the priorities for ECM on the school improvement plan, and those on the ECM development plan.

Table 1.1 provides a useful checklist for the manager of ECM to utilise with the link governor for ECM in order to check progress towards meeting the statutory requirements and duties of the governing body in relation to ECM.

The link governor for ECM will need to know the following in relation to ECM in the school:

- How is the school identifying pupils who require the common assessment framework (CAF) process?
- How many pupils in school this year have gone through the CAF process?
- What has been the impact of any staff CPD for ECM on improving their practice?
- How effective is the school's ECM team in moving ECM policy and practice forward?
- Are there any pupils in the school who are achieving poor ECM outcomes and, if so, what is being done to narrow the gaps and improve outcomes?
- How are external partnerships contributing to the delivery of ECM and the improvement of the five outcomes?
- What are the school-level indicators for pupil well-being telling you?
- How is teaching and learning impacting on the ECM outcomes and vice versa?

Table 1.1 Governors' roles and responsibilities for ECM

ECM outcomes	Governors' roles and responsibilities	Fully met?
Be healthy	Ensure the school meets health and safety requirements and keeps its health and safety policy under regular review	
	Ensure pupils participate in at least two hours of PE per week	
	Promote an ethos that encourages the participation of all pupils in competitive sport within and between schools	
	Monitor nutritional standards within school to ensure all meals, snacks and food available in school is healthy and nutritious	
	Ensure a whole-school drugs policy has been developed and is in place	
	Agree on the content and organisation of the school's programme for sex and relationships education (SRE) and notify parents of their right to withdraw the child from SRE	
	Monitor pupils' attitudes, values and how their personal qualities are developed within the school and through the provision of RE and PSHCE	
	Ensure the effective inclusion and integration of those children from minority ethnic groups, with SEN/LDD, EAL, refugee and asylum seekers	
	Support pupils in developing a sense of pride in their personal, cultural and linguistic identities	
	Ensure the school promotes pupils' well-being in accordance with the Education and Inspections Act 2006	
	Ensure the school is working towards or has achieved the Healthy Schools Status	
Stay safe	Consider the provision of sex and drugs education and ensure sex education is provided (in the case of the secondary school)	
	Ensure the school building is safe and secure and accessible to the disabled	
	Ensure the school is fulfilling its responsibilities regarding child protection and safeguarding	
	Ensure the school's health and safety policy is kept under regular review and that all health and safety legislation and precautions are followed	
	Ensure the school has an anti-bullying policy and behaviour policy in place which are both regularly reviewed, and ensure the correct procedures are followed for dealing with any racist or oppressive behavioural incidents	
	Ensure all pupils are cared for, guided and supported	

continued

From: *Implementing the Every Child Matters Strategy*, Routledge © Rita Cheminais 2010

Photocopiable
Resource

Table 1.1 continued

ECM outcomes	Governors' roles and responsibilities	Fully met?
Enjoy and achieve	Ensure high standards of educational achievement and that every child reaches their optimum potential	
	Monitor the school's performance against the targets set for achievement at KS1, KS2, KS3, KS4	
	Monitor the achievement of any under-achieving groups of pupils and the impact of policies on race, SEN and disability, EAL, LAC, FSM	
	Ensure every child receives the full statutory curriculum that the school must provide and that the time allowances for the subjects is met	
	Ensure the school has a curriculum policy and a teaching and learning policy that meets the pupils' needs and reflects personalised learning approaches	
	Set attendance targets and monitor the school's performance against these targets	
	Ensure that parents and carers receive an annual report on their child's educational achievement	
	Ensure the school has policies on race equality, SEN and disability, and equal opportunities and that they are reviewed regularly and assessed for their impact on pupils, staff and parents	
	Receive reports on the quality of teaching and learning and the progress of pupils in the school	
	Ensure a performance management policy is in place and monitor its implementation; conduct the performance management of the headteacher	
	Monitor the provision of extra-curricular, extended school activities for all groups of pupils, including residential experiences to promote pupils' recreational and social development	
	Ensure that the school challenges and prevents racism and discrimination, promotes good race relations and prepares pupils for living in a multicultural and diverse society	
	Monitor exclusion rates by gender, ethnicity, FSM, and SEN and take appropriate action on any disproportionate outcomes	

From: *Implementing the Every Child Matters Strategy*, Routledge © Rita Cheminais 2010

Photocopiable Resource

ECM outcomes	Governors' roles and responsibilities	Fully met?
Make a positive contribution	Ensure the school has an effective behaviour and anti-bullying policy. Monitor the implementation of these policies and their impact on individuals and groups of pupils	
	Monitor the development of pupils' attitudes, values, personal qualities and pupil voice	
	Ensure the aims and values for the school are agreed and that a positive ethos for the school is promoted. Also ensure that policy decisions are consistent with the agreed aims, values and ethos	
	Ensure that the school has an effective school council which reflects the full diversity of the pupil population, and that it informs school decision-making and has a voice that is listened to	
	Ensure the school promotes inclusive policies that allow for the achievement of all pupils	
	Ensure that adequate provision is made for transitions between children's centre and primary school, primary and secondary education, and secondary education and FE/HE	
	Ensure the school meets its duty under the Race Relations Amendment Act 2000 and fulfils its statutory responsibility in terms of equalities, as required by the SEF	
	Support initiatives to promote race equality and community cohesion	
	Ensure the teaching of PSHCE and the SEAL programme enable pupils to develop empathy, tolerance, and life skills as future citizens	
Achieve economic well-being	Ensure the quality of education, teaching and learning promote high standards	
	Ensure that standards of achievement continue to rise and monitor the school's performance	
	Monitor how out-of-hours provision/extended school activities contribute to enabling pupils to achieve economic well-being	
	Ensure that the 14–19 curriculum is broad, balanced and provides for vocational training, as well as academic qualifications	
	Ensure that all pupils in the secondary phase of education have access to careers advice	
	Ensure the school works well with the community, parents and other schools	
	Monitor the impact of school policies and plans on the achievement of minority ethnic groups, including Traveller and Looked After Children (LAC)	
	Ensure the school works effectively with other agencies to support vulnerable children and their families, including those from refugee, asylum seeking and Traveller backgrounds	

From: *Implementing the Every Child Matters Strategy*, Routledge © Rita Cheminais 2010

The Training and Development Agency for Schools (TDA), in their *School Improvement Planning Framework* (2008) module *Beyond the Classroom*, focuses on ECM and ways to improve pupil well-being through extended services and other provision. It offers some 'tough' questions on school leaders and managers of ECM that the link governor for ECM should be seeking the answers to. These are:

- Do you know how external partners can extend your school's ability to affect ECM outcomes?
- Does your improvement plan address the well-being of your children and young people?
- Does your improvement plan integrate ECM outcomes with your learning priorities?
- Is there a clear, evidence-based statement of how the school is contributing specifically to each of the ECM outcomes?

(TDA 2008: 54)

The role of the school's children's workforce and ECM

Schools are not expected to deliver the five ECM outcomes alone. They promote and improve pupils' ECM well-being through working in partnership with external agencies. This has resulted in a wider children's workforce being present in schools, of which teachers, teaching assistants and learning mentors make up only one part, with practitioners from health, social care, youth justice services, the police, Connexions and voluntary community organisations forming the other.

The manager of ECM in school will find helpful the *Inter-professional Values Underpinning Work with Children and Young People Joint Statement* (2007) agreed between the Nursing and Midwifery Council (NMC), the General Social Care Council (GSCC) and the General Teaching Council for England (GTC). It states:

> Children's practitioners … share responsibility for a range of outcomes for children. They are committed to ensuring all children have the chance to: be healthy, stay safe, enjoy and achieve, make a positive contribution, and experience economic well-being.

> Practitioners concern themselves with the whole child, whatever their specialism.

The Professional Standards for Teachers' Qualified Teacher Status also confirms:

> All the standards are underpinned by the five key outcomes for children and young people identified in Every Child Matters and the six areas of the Common Core of skills and knowledge for the children's workforce.

The six areas of the common core of skills and knowledge for the children's workforce are:

1 Effective communication and engagement with children, young people, their families and carers.
2 Child and young person development.
3 Safeguarding and promoting the welfare of the child.
4 Supporting transitions.
5 Multi-agency working.
6 Sharing information.

The TDA, in their *Guidance on the National Occupational Standards for Supporting Teaching and Learning in Schools: Overview of Policy and Initiatives* (2007), also show how these national standards, which are relevant to teaching assistants and other non-teaching staff in schools, link with ECM outcomes and the common core of skills and knowledge for the children's workforce. In a nutshell, the school's wider children's workforce's key roles and responsibilities for ECM are to:

- safeguard and promote the welfare of children and young people;
- identify and remove barriers to learning and participation;
- promote and contribute to the improvement of children and young people's ECM well-being;
- act as a champion for children and young people;
- promote and encourage pupil voice;
- focus on the impact of their interventions in improving a child or young person's ECM outcomes;
- contribute towards helping to improve children and young people's life chances;
- support and contribute to the provision of extended school provision.

The manager of ECM in school also needs to ensure that ECM is at the heart of the CPD programme for the wider children's workforce and demonstrates clearly how each CPD activity links to each of the five ECM outcomes. This approach will also align with the performance management system for school staff, which has an objective relating to ECM.

Developing the ECM vision, policy and charter

The government's ECM programme offers a sweeping vision about children and young people's entitlements to having a good life. A vision statement is a declaration of a shared sense of purpose about ECM. It is expressed as ideas about what ECM will be like in the future. The vision is intended to be powerful, inspiring and motivational, and can be a short statement that is easy to remember and follow, or a more comprehensive explanation of a preferred future for ECM. While there is no blueprint for what a shared vision statement should look like for ECM, there are some key questions to be considered when undertaking a visioning exercise with a range of stakeholders. These initial key questions are:

- Where are we now? (The school's current position on ECM.)
- What is coming up? (Any emerging ECM issues or impacts affecting the school.)
- Where do we want to be? (What is our shared vision for ECM?)
- How are we going to get there? (Required actions and resources needed.)

In addition to these questions, it may be helpful to provide a lead-in activity, based on stakeholders completing the following statement:

Every Child Matters in this school because ...

The entire visioning process, led by the manager of ECM, will involve stakeholders in brainstorming, insightful questioning, creativity and innovation.

Producing a whole-school vision statement for ECM is a vital first step in strategic planning for ECM. Three examples of whole-school vision statements for ECM are illustrated below.

Excellence for all children in learning and well-being.

Building a brighter future through Every Child Matters.

Every child's learning, happiness, safety, health and well-being matters in Leafy Lane School.

Developing a school ECM policy

The manager of ECM will need to engage a range of key stakeholders in developing the school policy for ECM. This collaborative process is best undertaken by a working party that includes representatives from the governing body, the headteacher, staff, parents/carers, school council and external agencies.

Once the school policy for ECM has been drafted, consulted upon, amended and finalised, it will need to be approved and ratified by the governing body before it becomes fully operational.

The ECM policy will guide ECM provision and practice across the school. It should be reviewed annually and updated as new government policy and legislation is introduced. Other key school policies should have an opening statement that reflects the ECM outcomes.

Figure 1.5 provides a generic model of a school policy for ECM. It can be tailored and customised to suit the phase and context of the school.

Developing a charter for ECM

The manager of ECM is advised to work with members of the school council, the link governor for ECM and the headteacher to produce a pupils' charter for ECM. The charter, displayed in classrooms and around the school, helps to embed ECM. Figure 1.6 provides an example of an ECM pupil charter that can be adapted.

Provision management and mapping for ECM

Provision management is a strategic approach to enable schools to plan and record, as well as to identify any gaps existing in their additional ECM provision. The process involves gathering information about the impact of that additional ECM provision on improving pupils' well-being outcomes. Provision management enables the manager of ECM in school to analyse and evaluate the cost effectiveness and added value of the additional provision. ECM provision management is a key part of the school improvement process, which informs target setting and the school development plan priorities for ECM. It helps the school to evaluate its additional provision, pupils' ECM well-being outcomes, as well as the factors which contribute to improving these outcomes.

Provision mapping for ECM is a valuable and useful whole-school strategic planning tool which helps the manager of ECM to plan systematically to meet the identified pupils' well-being needs. A provision map provides an at-a-glance menu of all the additional provision and interventions the school offers its pupils in order to improve and promote their ECM well-being outcomes. Additional provision on the map is costed and listed under each of the five ECM outcomes. Table 1.2 offers a blank ECM provision map template that can be adapted.

The ECM provision map enables the manager of ECM to audit the needs of pupils and to systematically plan how best to use the school's resources. It also helps to identify any trends, patterns or gaps in ECM provision. The map provides robust information that enables the manager to make well-informed strategic decisions about how the school promotes and contributes to improving pupils' ECM well-being outcomes.

The provision map for ECM should be kept up-to-date and reviewed regularly, for example, at least once every term. Some schools hold an ECM consultation day once per term, where parents/carers, pupils, key school staff and those from external agencies review provision for the whole-school ECM provision map. It is important that the provision map links to the school improvement plan priorities for ECM, as well as with the self-evaluation form (SEF). The ECM provision map should be in an accessible format that is easily understood and interpreted by a range of different stakeholders, e.g. governors, staff, parents, OFSTED, external agencies and the LA.

Statement of principle

Leafy Lane School ensures that through its accessible, good-quality personalised learning, and extended school services and activities, every child matters and everyone feels valued as a member of a culturally diverse, enriching and inclusive learning community.

We believe the leisure activities, lifelong learning opportunities and the wrap-around care and personalised services on offer to pupils, families and the community promote a real sense of belonging and achievement in fulfilling the Every Child Matters five outcomes for children: being healthy, staying safe, enjoying and achieving, making a positive contribution, and achieving economic and social well-being.

This policy was developed in consultation and agreed with staff, governors, pupils, parents/carers and partners from multi-agency services, voluntary and community sector organisations.

Aims

The school aims to:

- promote an ethos of belonging to the school and the wider local community;
- develop a sense of respect and responsibility among children, young people and adults within the school;
- enable all pupils to reach their optimum potential through the delivery of barrier-free personalised learning and personalised services which meet a diversity of needs;
- provide well coordinated wrap-around care and extended services to support pupils and families in the community;
- provide an appropriate range of enriching, interesting and relevant out-of-school-hours learning activities that respond to identified needs;
- develop collaborative and productive partnerships with other schools, external agencies, voluntary and community organisations in order to deliver the ECM outcomes;
- promote the achievement and well-being of pupils, families and the community accessing the extended services;
- work in partnership with parents/carers to enable them to support the learning and well-being of their child;
- demonstrate the value-added progress on the five ECM outcomes in the school-level indicators for pupil well-being, in addition to the use of appropriate assessment such as the Pupil Attitude to Self and School (PASS), Personal and Social Development scales, the Emotional and Behavioural Development scale, and the Personal, Social, Health Education and Citizenship assessment criteria;
- challenge discrimination and celebrate diversity.

Figure 1.5 ECM model school policy

From: *Implementing the Every Child Matters Strategy*, Routledge © Rita Cheminais 2010

Objectives

Being healthy

Ensure pupils:

- engage with the Healthy Schools and SEAL programmes to enjoy a healthy lifestyle and good well-being;
- participate in PE and other forms of sport and exercise;
- eat and drink healthily within school;
- benefit from on-site health and social care services to support their emotional, mental and physical well-being;

Staying safe

Ensure pupils are:

- safe, free from bullying, harassment and discrimination
- provided with a safe environment in which to develop, learn, play and socialise with others.

Enjoying and achieving

Ensure pupils:

- experience good-quality, fully inclusive teaching and learning;
- actively participate in enjoyable, relevant, interesting learning and recreational activities within and beyond the school day;
- regularly attend and enjoy school;
- review their own progress and any additional provision, which includes tailored teaching, catch-up or extension activities;
- are well-supported during periods of transition and transfer between and within schools.

Making a positive contribution

Ensure pupils:

- engage in decision-making, good behaviour, develop positive relationships, self-confidence and can manage change in their lives;
- have the opportunity to take responsibility in school, e.g. peer mentor, study buddy, peer mediator, prefect, form representative on school council;
- have a say in how the extended school and its related services operate;
- have the opportunity to participate in activities within the local community and between other schools;
- are well-supported in developing socially and emotionally.

Achieving economic well-being

Ensure pupils:

- have the opportunity to participate in 'Young Enterprise' activities;
- acquire key skills in relation to communication, team work, cooperative learning, financial awareness, problem solving and work related learning.

Figure 1.5 continued

Concept of ECM

ECM, the government's Change for Children programme, identifies that pupil performance and well-being go hand in hand. Children and young people cannot learn effectively if they do not feel safe or if health problems create barriers to learning.

ECM protects, nurtures and improves the life chances of children and young people, particularly of those who are vulnerable or at risk of underachieving.

The five well-being outcomes of ECM: (being healthy, staying safe, enjoying and achieving, making a positive contribution, and achieving economic well-being) are central to ensuring that effective joined-up children's services from education, health and social care are provided on or near the site of the school.

The school ensures that the ECM outcomes for children are delivered, as part of the Children Act 2004. The policy also meets the duty to promote pupil well-being, in accordance with the Education and Inspections Act 2006.

Relationship with other policies

- Extended school policy
- Inclusion policy
- Equal opportunities policy
- Admissions policy
- Safeguarding/child protection policy
- SEN and disability policy
- Behaviour and anti-bullying policies
- Health and safety policy
- Personal, social, health education and citizenship policies
- Personalised learning policy.

Coordination

The headteacher and the governing body have responsibility for ensuring that the ECM policy is fully implemented.

The assistant headteacher, as manager of ECM, has overall responsibility for coordinating, monitoring and evaluating the effectiveness of the ECM policy and provision throughout the school. He/she oversees the five key staff designated with responsibility for leading the whole-school implementation, monitoring and review of one of the allocated five ECM outcomes. The assistant headteacher responsible for ECM reports on pupils' progress towards meeting the five ECM outcomes, as well as on the ECM priorities in the school development plan, to the headteacher and the governing body. All teaching and non-teaching staff, including practitioners from multi-agency services, working with pupils within the school are responsible for ensuring pupils achieve positive outcomes in relation to learning and well-being.

Figure 1.5 continued

From: *Implementing the Every Child Matters Strategy*, Routledge © Rita Cheminais 2010

Resources

The school allocates a proportion of the Dedicated Schools Grant to support the delivery of the ECM outcomes and the implementation of the policy.

The budget for ECM is reviewed at the end of each financial year, following best-value principles.

Professional development

The school's continuing professional development programme is linked to the five ECM outcomes. School staff and multi-agency practitioners participate in joint inter-professional development activities each year. All courses and conferences attended by school staff in relation to ECM are evaluated for the impact they have on their work with pupils within and outside the classroom.

Implementation

- Specific attention will be paid to identifying and meeting the needs of pupils who are achieving poorly on the ECM outcomes.
- Staff will be sensitive to the needs of the whole child, and to relevant community issues.
- The school will promote pupil well-being within the school and in the wider local community.
- Pupils will be encouraged to share their worries and fears in an emotionally secure environment, with trusting adults.
- Information to parents/carers and the local community on ECM will be produced in an accessible range of alternative formats and languages.

Monitoring and Review

The Every Child Matters policy will be reviewed annually at the end of each academic year, to assess its effectiveness on pupils' well-being outcomes. Policy evaluation will focus on: establishing how far the aims and objectives of the policy have been met; how effectively resources have been allocated to meet the ECM outcomes; the progress pupils have made towards achieving the five ECM well-being outcomes; as well as seeking the views of parents/carers, pupils, staff and other key stakeholders. In light of all this evidence, the policy will be revised accordingly.

Key Dates

Ratification of the policy

Headteacher signature: _____ Date: _____

Chair of Governors signature: _____ Date: _____

Policy implemented on: _____ Policy review date: _____

Figure 1.5 continued

From: *Implementing the Every Child Matters Strategy*, Routledge © Rita Cheminais 2010

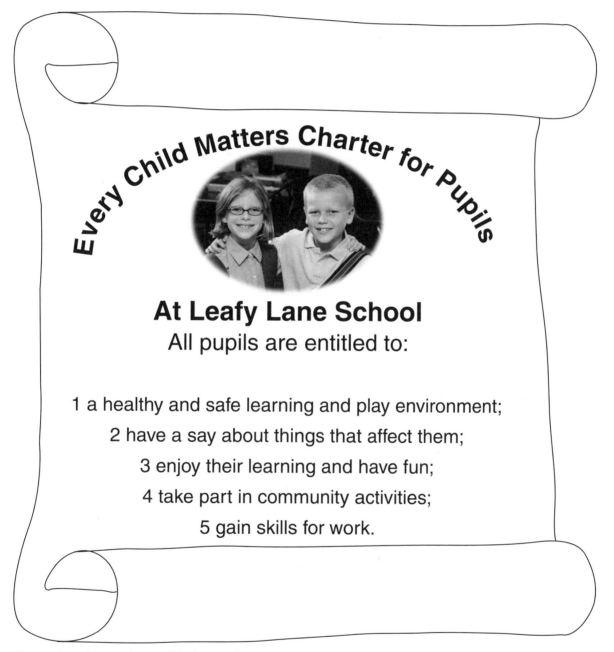

Every Child Matters Charter for Pupils

At Leafy Lane School
All pupils are entitled to:

1 a healthy and safe learning and play environment;

2 have a say about things that affect them;

3 enjoy their learning and have fun;

4 take part in community activities;

5 gain skills for work.

Figure 1.6 A sample pupils' charter for ECM

From: *Implementing the Every Child Matters Strategy*, Routledge © Rita Cheminais 2010

Table 1.2 Template for an ECM provision map

School: Term:

ECM outcomes	Year group and nature of need	Provision type and duration	Staff/pupil ratio	Staff/agencies delivering	Weekly cost in time (hrs)	Total annual cost (£)
Be healthy						
Stay safe						
Enjoy and achieve						
Positive contribution						
Economic well-being						

The key benefits of provision management and provision mapping are that it:

- ensures provision for ECM is equitable across the school;
- helps to address any gaps in ECM provision;
- identifies any potential underachievement in the ECM outcomes;
- helps to identify any staff professional development needs for ECM;
- helps to meet a range of statutory accountability requirements for ECM.

There are seven steps in the ECM provision management and mapping cycle. These are illustrated in Figure 1.7.

The system of provision management and provision mapping for ECM enables the manager of ECM to respond to the following key questions:

- Which additional provision to meet each of the five ECM outcomes is working well and why?
- Which additional provision for each of the five ECM outcomes is not working as well, why not, and how could this be addressed or improved?
- How do those delivering additional provision for ECM know that their interventions are making a positive impact on improving pupils' well-being?
- What is the pupil-level ECM outcomes data telling you about the impact and effectiveness of the additional provision available in the school?
- How well does the current additional provision for ECM match pupils' identified needs?
- What are the entry and exit criteria for the ECM provision map?
- What, if any, modifications need to be made to the current ECM provision map?

Budget allocation for ECM

Schools have to comply with the Financial Management Standards in Schools (FMSiS). The school budget needs to be used flexibly to support the delivery of the five ECM outcomes for pupils.

The Dedicated Schools Grant (DSG) is the main source of income in the school's budget. This DCSF government grant is allocated by the LA according to pupil numbers, as recorded in January from the Schools Census, and is adjusted by the LA in June, to reflect any changes in pupil numbers within the school.

Schools are also allocated additional funding within the DSG as top-ups for personalisation and special educational needs (SEN). This additional funding is designed to support the universal roll-out of a personalised offer to all pupils, including those with SEN, and is allocated on the basis of the numbers of pupils aged between five and fifteen. The personalisation and SEN funding needs to take into consideration the government's priorities each year, which include:

- ensuring all pupils are making good progress;
- early intervention to prevent pupils from falling behind;
- targeted support for specific groups of pupils, i.e. certain ethnic minorities, white working class, free-school-meals pupils, children in care and those with SEN;
- ensuring that the school workforce has the skills and confidence to address the needs of pupils with additional needs.

Schools are also likely to receive other specific grants, dependent on the schools standards and context. For example:

- Exceptional Circumstances Grant – allocated to schools with a rapid growth in pupil numbers due to a significant influx of, for example, English as an Additional Language (EAL) children.

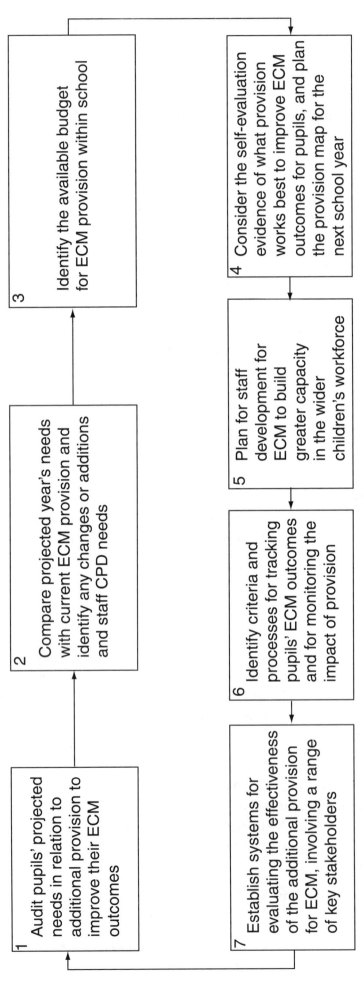

Figure 1.7 The stages in ECM provision management and mapping

1   Audit pupils' projected needs in relation to additional provision to improve their ECM outcomes

2   Compare projected year's needs with current ECM provision and identify any changes or additions and staff CPD needs

3   Identify the available budget for ECM provision within school

4   Consider the self-evaluation evidence of what provision works best to improve ECM outcomes for pupils, and plan the provision map for the next school year

5   Plan for staff development for ECM to build greater capacity in the wider children's workforce

6   Identify criteria and processes for tracking pupils' ECM outcomes and for monitoring the impact of provision

7   Establish systems for evaluating the effectiveness of the additional provision for ECM, involving a range of key stakeholders

- School Development Grant – allocated according to the level of social deprivation.
- Additional Standards Fund Grant – extra funding for government initiatives, e.g. Making Good Progress, to address pupil progression issues; extended schools sustainability; early years – extending and increasing the flexibility of the entitlement for 3–4 year olds; Playing for Success; music provision; School Lunch Grant.

The school's manager of ECM needs to liaise and work closely with the headteacher and the school's finance officer or bursar in order to establish how much funding from the school's budget can be allocated to support the delivery of the five ECM outcomes. The school's ECM provision map will record the amount of money allocated to all the different extra interventions and provisions to support pupils identified with a wide range of additional learning and well-being needs. This includes Wave 2 provision for small group 'catch-up' and 'stretch' interventions, such as ELS, ALS and FLS, Springboard Maths, additional in-class support from teaching assistants for SEN pupils, breakfast and homework clubs, sports coaching, nurture group provision, learning mentors, bilingual assistants, and art and drama therapists. Wave 3 additional provision is tailored to meet the needs of individual pupils with more complex needs and includes one-to-one specialist interventions, e.g. bereavement counselling, behaviour management, anger management, social skills and self-esteem programmes, and specialist multi-sensory programmes. The most effective additional interventions are those that last for 8–20 weeks.

Resourcing ECM

The school manager of ECM will need to oversee the ECM budget at a strategic level (provision management and mapping), as well as at an operational level (department allocations). The aim of budget allocation for ECM at either level is to secure best value, and to demonstrate the value added in relation to raising standards and improving pupils' well-being outcomes. In order to ensure that resources for supporting the delivery of the ECM outcomes at an operational level are allocated equitably across the school, the manager of ECM will request that each department submits an annual ECM resource application in February. This will be given consideration in respect of the impact that the resource(s) will have on improving pupils' ECM outcomes. The departmental application must address the ECM priorities on the department's development plan, which in turn reflect the school improvement plan priorities for ECM. Figure 1.8 provides a model template for putting together a departmental ECM resource application.

Seeking financial sponsorship for ECM projects

The school manager of ECM is expected to explore and seek external sponsorship opportunities in order to fund small-scale ECM projects designed to support and enhance the delivery of the ECM outcomes.

It is expected that the manager of ECM will prepare a project proposal, which will be approved by the headteacher and the governing body, before being submitted to the external sponsor. Figure 1.9 provides a template for an ECM project proposal.

Development planning for ECM

The school improvement plan priorities can either be organised according to each of the five ECM outcomes, or the plan can have one ECM priority, with a series of activities to address meeting all five outcomes. Either model is acceptable, but the first approach is best practice, as it will align more closely with the school budget allocation, the school SEF, and with the

Every Child Matters resource application

Department: _____ **Date submitted:** _____

Please indicate below one Every Child Matters priority for your department in the next academic year. Justify the priority and indicate the expected impact on pupils ECM outcomes.

ECM Priority: _____

_____

Justification: _____

_____

Expected impact: _____

_____

In the table below please indicate the resource(s) you wish to purchase to meet the ECM priority identified, outlining briefly how it will support staff development for Every Child Matters.

Resource description	Cost of the resource for ECM	Resource supplier	Contribution to staff ECM CPD	ECM outcome(s) being supported	Link to SDP and the SEF

Head of Department: _____

Manager of ECM: _____ **Date approved:** _____

Figure 1.8 Model ECM departmental resource application

Every Child Matters project proposal

School: _____

Project title: _____

_____

Project aim: _____

Project objectives: _____

_____

_____

Expenditure breakdown:

Total expenditure: £_____

Timescale for project: _____

Nominated sponsor: _____

ECM project proposer: _____

Date of project submission: _____

Signature of project proposer: _____

Signature of headteacher: _____

Figure 1.9 Model ECM project proposal template

school-level indicators for pupil well-being. Designing and framing the school improvement plan around the ECM outcomes helps staff to make the connection between ECM and standards.

Departmental subject or aspect development plans will also need to include a priority relating to ECM. The manager of ECM will need to produce an ECM development plan in order to support the implementation of the whole-school policy and provision for ECM. The priorities of this plan will have been identified following an audit for ECM. The Every Child Matters Standards framework, for example, provides a useful audit tool for reviewing current ECM policy and practice. This is centred on 12 ECM themes, and the audit will help to identify the key priorities and gaps existing in ECM, that need to be addressed. Further information about the Every Child Matters Standards can be found at www.ecm-solutions.org.uk.

A good ECM development plan should:

* be based on robust evidence gathered from a variety of sources and stakeholders;
* be clearly focused on raising standards in learning and well-being;
* acknowledge the financial implications;
* make explicit the intended outcomes;
* identify responsibilities for achieving the intended outcomes;
* stipulate timescales;
* recognise the implications for staff professional development;
* state the success criteria for evaluating the outcomes.

The success criteria should be based on professional judgements about the present performance and future goals for ECM. It should be measurable, visible, ascertainable and challenging, and indicate clearly the required evidence to judge success.

The manager of ECM in school will need to keep the development plan for ECM under review, and feedback to the headteacher, governing body and staff on the progress made towards meeting the plan's ECM priorities. The manager will need to gather the views of pupils, parents/carers, staff, multi-agency practitioners; undertake classroom observations to see ECM in practice; observe extended school activities; sample teacher planning for ECM; and analyse pupil-level ECM well-being data. All these sources will enable the manager of ECM to judge how effective policy, provision and staff development has been in addressing the priorities on the ECM development plan. Table 1.3 provides an example of a development plan for ECM.

Whole-school target setting for ECM

There are no statutory targets relating directly to ECM. Therefore, schools are not compelled to set targets in relation to the five ECM outcomes. However, it is considered to be good practice to do so, particularly in view of the school-level indicators for pupil well-being, the renewed OFSTED inspection framework and SEF, and the forthcoming School Report Card, which records ECM in the 'wider outcomes' section.

The setting of optional additional targets for the ECM outcomes should be informed by the school's self-evaluation and improvement planning processes. The headteacher, the governing body and the manager of ECM should be evaluating the impact of ECM on pupils' achievement and progress, the effectiveness of the school's partnerships, the range of extended services available, and community cohesion. These are all key factors in contributing to supporting the delivery of the ECM outcomes within a school, and have a major influence on whole-school target setting for ECM.

Table 1.3 Example of a school's ECM development plan

ECM priorities	Actions/activities	Lead person(s)	Resources	Timescale	Monitoring	Success criteria
1 Developing and implementing an ECM policy	**a** Consult upon and draft ECM policy **b** Amend draft policy following consultation **c** Governors ratify ECM policy	ECM manager	Three days non-contact time for ECM manager	Start June 2010 and ratified September 2010	ECM manager gives updates on implementation and effectiveness of ECM policy to headteacher and governors	ECM policy informs everyday ECM practice
2 Introducing and embedding ECM across the curriculum	**a** Deliver whole-school INSET to introduce the QCA ECM document **b** Subject leaders to monitor ECM in their curriculum subject	Curriculum coordinator with ECM manager	One day for planning and delivering twilight INSET + three days for monitoring ECM across curriculum	Start summer term 2010 and embedded by July 2011	ECM manager and curriculum coordinator sampling teacher planning, and undertaking paired classroom observations	ECM embedded successfully across the curriculum
3 Producing a whole-school ECM provision map	**a** Bringing together all the different provisions for AEN pupils in one place **b** First draft of whole-school ECM provision map produced **c** Final ECM provision map produced and piloted	ECM manager with INCO and SENCO	Two days non-contact time to produce ECM provision map	Start June 2010 and completed by September 2010	ECM manager monitors and reviews ECM provision map each term from September 2010	ECM provision map indicates good value for money and added value in terms of supporting the delivery of the ECM outcomes
4 Organising the staff CPD programme to align with the ECM outcomes	**a** Staff CPD programme aligned with ECM outcomes **b** CPD evaluation forms revised to reflect ECM outcomes **c** Joint inter-professional training opportunities for ECM provided in-house	CPD Coordinator and ECM manager	Two days non-contact time to plan and evaluate ECM CPD programme Three one-hour twilights for joint inter-professional staff ECM CPD	Start September 2010 and reviewed in July 2011	CPD coordinator evaluates impact of ECM staff CPD with ECM manager through paired classroom observations, and scrutiny of staff CPD evaluation forms	School staff more confident and skilled in delivering the ECM outcomes and working in partnership with practitioners from multi-agencies

continued

Table 1.3 continued

	Actions	Who	Resources	Timescale	Monitoring	Success criteria
5 Working towards achieving the Every Child Matters Standards Award	a ECM Standards audit undertaken b Evidence gathered for the ECM portfolio c One-day external on-site assessment undertaken	ECM manager with the school's ECM team	One day to audit current ECM policy and practice Three days (one per term) to meet with ECM team to review progress One day for compiling portfolio of evidence Six one-hour ECM team meetings	Start September 2010 and completed by July 2011	ECM manager and the ECM team gather evidence to meet the 12 Every Child Matters Standards. Team meet with ECM manager each half term, to review progress towards meeting the Every Child Matters Standards ECM manager updates governors and headteacher on progress	School successfully achieves the Every Child Matters Standards Award within 12 months
6 Updating the school prospectus and school website to reflect the ECM outcomes	a Brainstorming ideas with ICT coordinator, ECM team and the School Council on new website and school prospectus linking to ECM outcomes b First initial designs produced and consulted upon c Final new revised website operating, and school prospectus printed and published	ECM manager and the ICT coordinator	Two days non-contact time for ICT coordinator to work on re-designing website Two days non-contact time for ECM manager and ICT coordinator to redesign school prospectus	Start June 2010 and completed by end of September 2010	ECM manager meets with ICT coordinator in June, July and September 2010 to review progress and advise on content and layout for ECM linkage	Positive feedback from staff, parents, pupils and external partners on the new school website aligned with ECM Positive comments from stakeholders on the new school prospectus and its alignment with the ECM outcomes

A good target for ECM should have a specific focus, which will be an area for development and improvement in relation to ECM. When setting whole-school targets for ECM there needs to have been established a baseline for the five ECM outcomes. There should be an element of realistic ambition and challenge in the ECM targets set, as well as agreed measures of success. The achievement of targets set for ECM helps to demonstrate the value-added progress made in relation to promoting and improving pupils' well-being outcomes. Table 1.4 provides an example of whole-school target setting in relation to the five ECM outcomes.

Information for the School Report Card on ECM

The School Report Card will replace the School Profile in 2011. It will provide an 'at-a-glance' overview of a school's standards and achievements overall, including performance against all five ECM outcomes. The 'wider outcomes' section on the School Report Card will indicate how a school is performing in relation to pupils' health, safety, enjoyment, opportunity and ability to make a positive contribution, and prospects of future economic well-being. It will reflect the school-level indicators for pupil well-being, which includes measures of attendance, persistent absences, exclusions, pupil behaviour, take-up of school lunches, take-up of PE and sport, as well as parents' and pupils' satisfaction surveys relating to the five ECM outcomes. Figure 1.10 provides an example of what the School Report Card is likely to comprise of.

Table 1.4 Example of whole-school targets for the ECM outcomes

Every Child Matters outcomes	End of Key Stage 3 targets 2010–2011
Be healthy	100% pupils undertake the SEAL programme 97% of pupils undertake two hours of PE or sport per week 87% of pupils eat a healthy school lunch
Stay safe	97% of pupils report they feel safe in school 3% or less reported incidents of bullying, racism or discrimination 100% of pupils accessing a key adult in school
Enjoy and achieve	97% attendance rate 3% reduction in number of persistent absentees 0% permanent exclusions 85% of pupils participate in extended school activities 92% pupils report they enjoy school 90% of pupils reach their personal best in the core subjects
Make a positive contribution	98% of pupils participate in a community, voluntary or fund-raising activity 100% of pupils have a 'voice' and engage in school decision-making processes
Achieve economic well-being	90% of pupils confident in relation to financial literacy 97% of pupils have an external workplace or local business enterprise experience 100% of pupils engage in team working

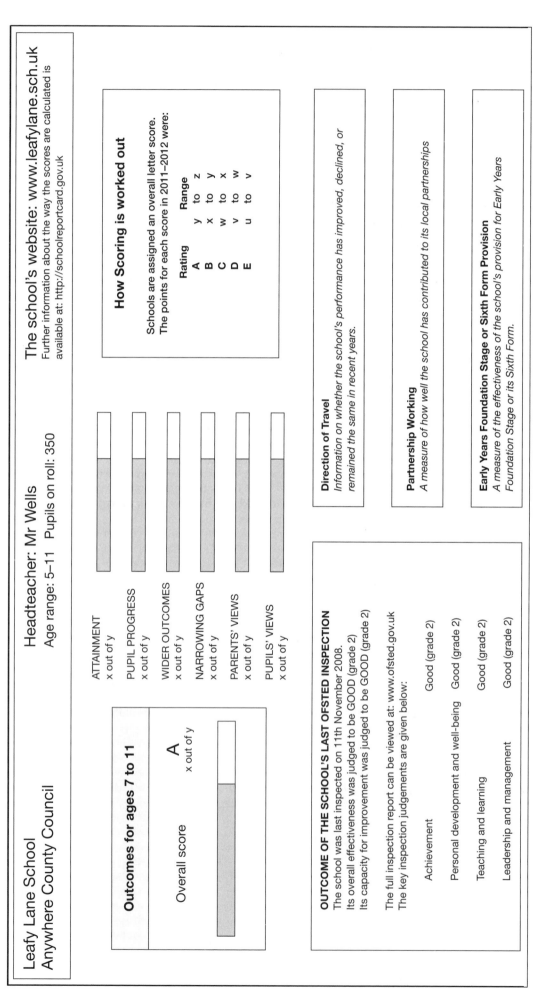

Figure 1.10 Example of the proposed School Report Card

Questions for further reflection

1 To what extent does the school consider the ECM outcomes as being part of its self-evaluation and improvement planning?

2 How far has CPD undertaken in the school had an impact on developing staff skills and confidence in ECM?

3 How is ECM focusing on particular groups of pupils in the school, e.g. gifted and talented, minority ethnic, white working class, FSM, SEN and disability, looked after children?

4 Are certain groups of pupils achieving poor ECM outcomes in comparison to others?

5 What procedures are in place within the school to promote the ECM well-being of pupils?

6 What does the school do to ensure there is good evidence for each of the five ECM outcomes?

7 What ECM priorities have been set for further development and why?

8 What are the strengths and weaknesses of ECM within the school?

9 Which ECM outcome(s) are considered to require further development in the school, and how will this be addressed?

10 What, if any, are the barriers to implementing ECM throughout the school, and how can these be removed?

11 What have been the advantages of linking the ECM outcomes to school provision and organisation?

2

Leading and Implementing the Every Child Matters Strategy

> **This chapter covers:**
>
> - the key features of the effective strategic leadership of Every Child Matters (ECM);
> - developing and overseeing the work of the ECM team in school;
> - leading teachers in the ECM outcomes;
> - useful frameworks for supporting the implementation of ECM in school;
> - questions for further reflection.

Key features of the effective strategic leadership of ECM

The term 'strategic' refers to knowing what to achieve, justifying the direction taken and finding the best ways to get there. The strategic leadership of ECM is rooted in school self-assessment, action planning, target setting and responding to, and acting upon, pupils' feedback about their well-being. Two important approaches enable the manager of ECM to implement ECM in the everyday practice within a school. These are:

- forging robust links between ECM, school improvement planning, self-evaluation and continuing professional development (CPD);
- using the ECM outcomes in a systematic way to plan strategies for school improvement.

The characteristics of effective strategic leadership for ECM includes:

- the continual drive for further improvement in relation to pupil well-being;
- a determination to avoid complacency;
- strong team work for ECM;
- an agreed sense of common purpose, i.e. the five ECM outcomes provide the common goals and moral purpose.

According to the research undertaken by Mary Atkinson *et al.* (2008) on behalf of the National College for School Leadership (NCSL) now known as the National College for Leadership of Schools and Children's Services, there are six key messages for those leading ECM in a school. These messages are:

1 To be able to convince school staff, governors, parents and carers that ECM complements and helps to raise school standards, because it focuses on meeting the needs of the whole child in overcoming barriers to learning and participation.
2 The ECM agenda is a collective responsibility, and requires a broad range of individuals to take on shared leadership roles for ECM outcomes in a school.
3 Partnership working within, and beyond, the school is essential to supporting the delivery of the ECM outcomes.

4 Taking a wider outward-looking view in helping to transform the community through adopting system leadership is important in relation to enhancing the ECM outcomes and the life chances of children and young people locally.

5 Consultation with pupils, parents/carers and the wider community is essential in order to develop more responsive solutions to ECM that meet local needs.

6 New skills are required by school leaders and managers of ECM. For example: relationship building, negotiation, brokerage, commissioning, emotional intelligence and entrepreneurism.

Developing and overseeing the work of the ECM team

ECM is at the heart of workforce remodelling, and the staff most likely to be engaged in ECM are not teachers. Staffing structures for ECM feature distributed leadership, which helps to spread responsibility for ECM across all levels of the workforce. This enables staff such as learning mentors, teaching assistants and higher level teaching assistants (HLTAs) to have the demands of ECM reflected in their job descriptions and person specifications. New roles have been created for such staff, which includes pastoral managers, family liaison workers, community champion, home–school liaison worker and extended school coordinator. Pupils and parents may also take on leadership roles for aspects of ECM through the school council and the parents council.

Distributed leadership and team building for ECM are powerful forms of staff CPD, which both help to build capacity within the school. Integrating ECM into the working practices and performance management process for school staff ensures that this important strategy is not perceived as a bolt-on initiative.

The formation of a school team for ECM is a key means of driving and embedding ECM throughout the school. The headteacher and the senior manager of ECM can nominate team members to implement and develop specific ECM outcomes. Teaching and learning responsibility (TLR) posts can help to facilitate the ECM distributed leadership model among teaching staff who take on a specific role for ECM. The leading teachers for each of the five ECM outcomes are also important members of the ECM school team. Practitioners from external agencies may become associate members of the ECM team – for example, the school nurse. Figure 2.1 illustrates a school's ECM team structure.

The manager of ECM oversees and guides the work of the ECM team. He or she meets with the team formally every half-term. This team will undertake activities to meet the identified priorities on the school development plan for ECM. The ECM manager will monitor and evaluate the impact of the team's work in supporting the delivery of the ECM outcomes.

The ECM team publish updates in the school's weekly bulletin to keep staff abreast of ECM developments. The school council and parent council link directly into the ECM team. The ECM team work closely with staff to help them develop ideas to include in their teaching. ECM activity days for pupils are organised in partnership with the school council and the ECM team members.

Leading teachers in the ECM outcomes

It is good practice to nominate leading teachers in the ECM outcomes who can spearhead improvements in the competence and confidence of other teaching colleagues in supporting the delivery of the ECM outcomes. Depending on the size of the school, there may be one leading teacher for each of the five ECM outcomes, or there may be one or two leading teachers who each share two or three of the outcomes, or one leading teacher who supports the development of all five ECM outcomes throughout the school.

ECM Team

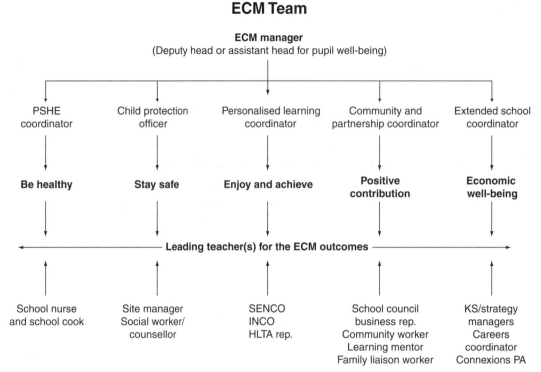

Figure 2.1 Example of a school ECM team structure

Leading teachers for ECM on the upper pay spine (UPS) within the school will have a TLR in view of the work they undertake in helping to embed ECM into everyday classroom practice. The leading teachers will be members of the school's core ECM team. The work of the leading teachers for ECM will help other teachers in the school to:

- identify when pupils' ECM well-being outcomes are poor, and when these may be causing a barrier to their learning;
- recognise the links between ECM outcomes and personalised learning;
- take a holistic view of every pupil's progress and achievements in relation to learning and well-being;
- assess pupils' progress in the ECM outcomes to the same extent as that in learning;
- know what procedures and services to refer pupils to who are achieving poor ECM outcomes;
- work collaboratively with other children's workforce practitioners in order to support the delivery of the ECM outcomes.

The role of the leading teacher in the ECM outcomes can be summarised as being to:

- support teachers' understanding and knowledge of the ECM outcomes;
- advise and support teachers on how to implement ECM across the curriculum, or in their specific curriculum subject;
- coach and mentor teachers in how to promote pupil well-being in the classroom in delivering the ECM outcomes;
- act as an advocate and champion for children's well-being;
- actively listen to teachers' concerns and issues about the delivery of ECM and provide constructive feedback on how to resolve problems;
- model effective classroom practice in the delivery of the ECM outcomes;
- support the induction of newly qualified or new teachers joining the school, in relation to ECM;
- support teachers in tracking, reviewing and assessing pupils' progress in the ECM outcomes;

- contribute to school in-service education and training (INSET) on ECM;
- signpost teachers to further sources of information on ECM;
- disseminate good practice in the delivery of ECM within the school's local learning networks and cluster groups.

Figure 2.2 gives a model job description for an ECM leading teacher.

Useful frameworks for supporting the implementation of ECM in school

There are several frameworks available to schools, which enable leaders and managers of ECM, to implement and embed ECM throughout the school. There are some that are more practical, useful and tried and tested than others. Three frameworks will be covered in this section of the chapter. These include:

- The Training and Development Agency for Schools (TDA) *School Improvement Planning Framework*.
- The NCSL *Levers for Leaders* and the accompanying *ECM Premium Project* and the *ECM Leadership Direct* online resources.
- The ECM Solutions *Every Child Matters Standards* framework, which has the potential to lead to a nationally validated award for schools, academies and pupil referral units (PRUs).

The TDA School Improvement Planning Framework

The TDA launched their *School Improvement Planning Framework* in autumn 2008, after an initial pilot in 2007. The framework is designed to help school leaders to make ECM a reality, by aligning raising standards with pupil well-being. It offers a suite of tools, practical ideas and resources to enable school leaders to raise awareness about ECM among key stakeholders, as well as helping them to prioritise ECM aims in the context of the whole-school improvement planning process. The section entitled: *Identify objectives: beyond the classroom* has a specific focus on ECM, and has two practical activities to undertake with staff and governors. The first is an ECM card-sort activity which focuses on raising awareness about ECM in order to help identify priority aims for the school and its partner agencies in relation to improving pupils' well-being through the delivery of the ECM outcomes.

The second activity is focused on using a solutions matrix to map existing and proposed activities for ECM inside and beyond the classroom, against the priority aims for delivering the ECM outcomes identified in the previous card-sort activity.

You can download the toolkit and accompanying resources from the following website: www.tda. gov.uk/remodelling/extendedschools/sipf2.aspx

The NCSL/TDA (2009) five-step process to meeting the ECM goals

The NCSL, renamed the National College for Leadership of Schools and Children's Services (NCLSCS), in partnership with the TDA, published its resource pack, *Engaging Schools in Sustainable Every Child Matters and Extended Services*, in May 2009. This essential resource for leaders and ECM managers in schools and other education settings comprises seven booklets: (1) Introduction; (2) Research and insights; (3) Diagnostic tool – understanding and engagement tool; (4) Coaching tool – introduction; (5) Coaching tool – levers of change: diagnostic wheel; (6) Coaching tool – running a 'working together' event; (7) Route map to support.

The resource pack is designed to help school leaders and ECM managers to develop extended services and meet the goals of ECM. The information in the pack is based on evidence from a

Photocopiable
Resource

Post Designation: Leading Teacher responsible for Every Child Matters

Responsible to: The Manager of Every Child Matters

Post grade: TLR1b

Effective from: 1st September 2010

Main duties and responsibilities:

1 To contribute to the school's overall response and commitment to delivering the Every Child Matters (ECM) outcomes.
2 To devise and implement intervention strategies within a framework of best practice for ECM.
3 To support teaching staff in implementing ECM across the curriculum.
4 To coach and mentor other teaching colleagues in implementing the SEAL programme.
5 To model good practice in supporting the delivery of the ECM outcomes in the classroom.
6 To assist teaching and support staff in assessing pupils' ECM outcomes.
7 To support the planning of whole-school ECM-themed pupil activity days.
8 To contribute to the NQT induction programme and to whole staff INSET.
9 To work with external partners to support the delivery of ECM outcomes.
10 To undertake collaborative projects for ECM to help build staff capacity.
11 To monitor and evaluate the impact and effectiveness of work undertaken.
12 To keep own CPD for ECM updated.

The post holder is required to meet the National Professional Standards for Threshold/Senior teachers and to comply with employment, health and safety, equal opportunities legislation, and undergo Enhanced Disclosure with the CRB.

The job description is current; it will be reviewed annually, and may be amended to reflect changes in job requirements, as commensurate with the grade of post.

Figure 2.2 Model job description for an ECM leading teacher

From: *Implementing the Every Child Matters Strategy*, Routledge © Rita Cheminais 2010

two-year partnership project, involving a sample of LAs, schools, the NCSL and the TDA. Although a five-step process is recommended, each component can be used separately in the resource pack. Table 2.1 illustrates the five-step process.

Table 2.1 The five-step process to meeting the ECM goals and the development of extended services

Step one Engage	Step two Mobilise leaders	Step three Mobilise others	Step four Work together	Step five Sustain progress
Resources				
Research and insights diagnostic tools	Coaching tools	Change lever diagnostic wheel	Running a working together event	Route map
Outcomes				
Understanding of what the ECM and ES agenda are about and where the school is now Curious to find out what is being offered.	Ready to participate, move to the next stage and engage in development	Greater understanding of what the issues are, who needs to be involved and who can support the work	Clear vision of what we will create, the sources of support available to us and an action plan to take the vision forward	Support received with solutions to make this change happen

From: NCSL/TDA (2009c) 1. Introduction, page 3 in *Engaging Schools in Sustainable Every Child Matters and Extended Services*.

School leaders and the ECM manager can work through the NCSL/TDA five-step process in the following ways:

Step 1

Research and insights: This helps school leaders, the ECM manager, school staff and governors to know what the barriers to implementing ECM and developing extended services (ES) are, and how to overcome these, based on findings from the research undertaken by the University of Warwick.

Diagnostic tool: This tool enables the school leader and the ECM manager to identify the school's strengths and weaknesses in relation to ten ECM/ES change indicators. Each change indicator has a series of prompt questions and four descriptors to support judgements relating to the school's current level of implementation of ECM and ES. This stage in the process promotes dialogue and engagement between key stakeholders in the school.

Step 2

Coaching tool: This introduces the coaching approach and model, which school leaders and ECM managers can utilise with staff and other partners/stakeholders to help them understand and manage the change process brought about by ECM and ES.

Step 3

Coaching tool: This focuses on six key levers for change illustrated by a diagnostic wheel, which is aimed at helping the school to take the right direction of travel towards developing an agreed vision and goals for ECM and ES. The six key levers cover: relevance; understanding; priorities; context; capacity; capability. A RAG rating system is utilised to help the school leader and ECM manager to evaluate the progress made in the change process. This tool helps stakeholders/partners to make the necessary cultural shift required for developing and implementing ECM/ES.

Step 4

Coaching tool: This focuses on running a working together workshop event. Its purpose is to help the school move its visions for ECM and ES towards a firm, agreed plan of action for implementation and development of both. The workshop engages governors, parents/carers, children/young people and external partners.

Step 5
Route Map: The route map provided in the resource pack must be used with the diagnostic tool and the diagnostic wheel. It signposts the school leader and the ECM manager to further NCSL and TDA resources. The purpose of the route map is to enable the school leader and the ECM manager to map relevant local provision for extended services to meet the ECM outcomes and goals. The NCSL/TDA resource pack can be ordered from: www.tda.gov.uk/about/publicationslisting/tda0672.aspx

The ECM Standards Framework

The ECM Standards self-evaluation framework comprises 12 standards covering the following aspects of ECM:

1 ethos
2 policy
3 environment
4 leadership and management
5 personalised learning
6 curriculum entitlement, access and choice

7 presence, participation and personal development
8 partnership with parents and carers
9 multi-agency working
10 community
11 transition and transfer
12 professional development.

Each ECM standard has a series of evidence descriptors aligned with the five ECM outcomes, which provide the judgement criteria for a school to ascertain its current position, and to identify any existing gaps that require further development.

The ECM Standards offer schools, academies and PRUs (short stay schools) the opportunity to achieve a national award in recognition of their good practice in ECM, providing they fulfil each standard at embedded level. The school collects and presents all the required evidence to meet the 12 standards in a portfolio, and undergoes a one-day on-site external assessment of ECM in action. The award is valid for three years, and can be renewed for a further three years upon reassessment. Further information about the ECM Standards and the award process can be obtained from: www.ecm-solutions.org.uk

Questions for further reflection

1 What opportunities and challenges does workforce remodelling for ECM pose to the school leader and the manager of ECM?
2 What are the advantages of linking the ECM outcomes to the school's organisation?
3 What are the implications for school leaders and managers of ECM in utilising all or one or two of the recommended frameworks for implementing ECM?
4 How will the ECM team be recruited and its purpose established in school?
5 What will the ECM manager do to publicise and raise awareness about the work of the school's ECM team?
6 How will the leading teacher(s) for ECM be identified and professionally developed to support the capacity building of other staff within the school?
7 What will be the benefits of linking the staff performance management and appraisal system to the ECM outcomes?
8 What support and guidance can the local authority and other independent external consultants offer the school to help them deliver the ECM outcomes?
9 How will the ECM manager ensure the governing body understands the role and responsibilities of the ECM leading teacher(s) and the school ECM team?

3

Every Child Matters and Personalised Learning

This chapter covers:

- understanding the links between Every Child Matters (ECM), personalisation and personalised learning;
- embedding ECM across the curriculum;
- school-level indicators for pupil well-being;
- tracking, recording and analysing pupils' progress in the ECM outcomes;
- engaging pupils in reviewing their own progress in the ECM outcomes;
- disseminating good practice in the ECM outcomes;
- questions for further reflection.

Understanding the links between ECM, personalisation and personalised learning

ECM was originally introduced for the purpose of bringing agencies together to safeguard children. It was not designed specifically to raise standards. ECM is about the whole child, whereas standards are about the school. ECM has become a universal entitlement for every child, as it is about doing things for all children, and not just for a few.

Before exploring the links between ECM, personalisation and personalised learning, it is helpful to define each of these concepts. ECM relates to five well-being outcomes: be healthy; stay safe; enjoy and achieve; make a positive contribution; and achieve economic well-being. These are all important in improving the life chances of children and young people.

Personalisation refers to children, young people and families as responsible service users and active participants, shaping and informing the development and delivery of education and related children's services.

Personalised learning embraces every aspect of school life, including: teaching and learning strategies; ICT; curriculum choice; organisation and timetabling; assessment arrangements; and relationships beyond the classroom with parents and the local community. It is the process of tailoring and matching teaching and learning around the way different pupils learn in order to meet their individual needs, interests and aptitudes to enable them to reach their optimum potential. Personalised learning is about enabling all children and young people to achieve the best they can through working in a way that suits them.

ECM goes hand-in-hand with personalisation and personalised learning because all three are dependent on understanding the needs of the whole child. All the ECM outcomes are intrinsic to an individual child's development, and are mutually reinforcing. They show the important relationship and inextricable link between educational achievement (standards) and the well-being of children and young people. For example, children and young people learn and thrive best when they are healthy, safeguarded from harm, free from poverty and engaged fully with school and learning. ECM helps to raise standards because it enables such barriers to learning to be overcome by schools working in partnership with other services such as health and social care.

Doing well in learning and education helps to boost children and young people's self-esteem and their emotional well-being. Effective personalised, tailored teaching and learning and extended school services not only help to raise children's and young people's attainment and achievement, but also influence other ECM outcomes such as by increasing their resilience and self-confidence, raising their aspirations and reducing disaffection.

The manager of ECM within a school needs to help staff see these links between the ECM outcomes, personalisation and personalised learning. Table 3.1 provides a useful point of reference for school staff to refer to. It should enable staff to see that schools have been contributing to improving and promoting children's ECM well-being outcomes for some time, prior to the introduction of the government's ECM agenda, and that ECM and standards do complement each other.

Table 3.1 ECM and personalising the school experience

ECM outcomes	School contributions to ECM outcomes	Personalising the school experience
Be healthy	▪ Encouraging children and young people to develop healthy and active lifestyles	School ethos and environment: ▪ School is pupil-focused and inclusive ▪ A robust behaviour policy and a clear rewards and sanctions system exists that enables pupils to feel safe and able to flourish in an emotionally intelligent environment ▪ A high-quality learning environment is provided with good-quality displays to showcase pupils' achievements
Stay safe	▪ Keeping children and young people safe from bullying, harassment, discrimination and harm	
Enjoy and achieve	▪ Ensuring each child and young person progresses as well as they can and attends school regularly	Adding value to learning: ▪ Curriculum entitlement and choice with the curriculum tailored to match the needs, interests and aptitudes of a diversity of pupils ▪ Assessment for learning and of pupils' progress, with pupils reviewing their own learning and progress ▪ Pupils acquiring the tools for learning and learning how to learn ▪ ICT exploited to enhance, extend and make learning accessible
Make a positive contribution	▪ Ensuring all children and young people have a 'voice' and participate in school decision-making, and are encouraged to volunteer to help others	Listening and talking to pupils: ▪ All pupils have a regular individual interview focused on their achievements, which makes good use of data, and involves the child's parents ▪ Pupils' views are sought on teaching and learning and well-being ▪ Pupils contribute to the life and work of the school ▪ Pupils learn how to become a responsible citizen
Achieve economic well-being	▪ Helping children and young people to value education and to appreciate that it is the key to success in later life	Supporting the whole child: ▪ Effective pastoral care providing guidance and support ▪ Multi-agency support ▪ Extended school activities ▪ Home–school and community partnerships

The manager of ECM in a school can also make reference to research into how ECM helps to raise standards. For example, recent research commissioned by the National College for School Leadership (NCSL) shows that a rise in standards of achievement and attainment is most likely to occur when:

- the ECM agenda is systematically pursued in a school through the development of a shared vision and a clear moral and educational purpose rooted in the ECM outcomes;
- workforce remodelling occurs which creates new roles and responsibilities across all levels of the staffing structure to address ECM and pupil well-being;
- empowering and helping parents and carers to support their child's learning and ECM well-being at home occurs;
- sustained and effective partnership working occurs with statutory and voluntary agencies to help remove barriers to learning and improve children's and young people's ECM well-being outcomes;
- curricular and non-curricular activities are categorised and evaluated against the five ECM outcomes;
- the five ECM outcomes are embedded and threaded across the curriculum;
- a good range of extended school activities are provided on site and/or between a cluster of schools.

Clearly, the broader strategy for promoting pupil well-being within the school helps to shape and advance the personalisation agenda considerably.

Embedding ECM across the curriculum

ECM is a fundamental part of the curriculum and its design, and is reflected in the national curriculum aims, which are to enable children and young people to become:
- successful learners who enjoy learning, make good progress and achieve their full potential;
- confident individuals who are able to lead safe, healthy and fulfilling lives;
- responsible citizens who make a positive contribution to society.

QCA, in their publication entitled *Every Child Matters at the Heart of the Curriculum*, comment:

> A curriculum underpinned by Every Child Matters requires passionate and committed teaching and offers opportunities for open-ended investigation, creativity, experimentation, team work, and performance. It should also involve real experiences, activities beyond the school, parental involvement, working with others in the community, recreational enjoyment, taking responsibility for events and activities and encountering challenging and unfamiliar contexts.
>
> (QCA 2008: 2)

The five ECM outcomes need to be built into every aspect of school life in order to become integral to, and reinforced through, every aspect of the curriculum. This includes: all subjects and lessons; key events such as sports day and concerts or community activities; the learning environment; and out-of-school-hours learning activities. The curriculum also promotes learners' well-being through the development of key skills essential for life which transfer across the curriculum. Teachers can colour-code and highlight the coverage of the ECM outcomes in their curriculum plans.

Many schools also adopt an integrated cross-curricular approach to all five ECM outcomes within individual learning experiences and across all aspects of school life by holding themed ECM outcomes activity days or an ECM well-being week. Table 3.2 illustrates examples of how the five ECM outcomes are incorporated in every national curriculum subject.

Table 3.2 ECM outcomes across the curriculum

	Be healthy	Stay safe	Enjoy and achieve	Make a positive contribution	Achieve economic well-being
What pupils need to learn	Importance of eating sensibly; staying physically active and getting enough rest; how to make positive choices and take sensible actions; how to protect their emotional, social and mental well-being; the long-term consequences of the lifestyle choices they make now	How to identify and minimise risk; how to make informed safe choices; how to voice their opinions and resist unhelpful peer pressure	How to work imaginatively and creatively to develop new ideas, insights and ways of doing things; how to assess their skills, achievements and potential in order to set personal goals and achieve their best; the joy to be gained from successful learning	To form positive relationships and avoid bullying and discriminatory behaviour; to learn about the different roles that people play in a community; how they can contribute to their own school and the wider community; how to work effectively with others	Learn about the global economy and how businesses work; the qualities and skills needed for adult working life; to be enterprising; how to manage their own money
Art and Design	Exploring and expressing personal concerns and emotions	Following safe practices in the working environment; forming and expressing opinions about art; exploring identity and place in the world	Participating in creative, meaningful and intelligent creation; expressing themselves in new and original ways; working in active learning environments	Collaborating with others on projects; exploring the role of art, craft and design across times and cultures	Developing skills in critical thinking and creative problem solving; learning about the creative industries; working with artists and designers
Citizenship	Being empowered through taking action and making decisions; learning about identity, diversity and respecting difference; learning about the politics of everyday life	Asking questions rather than taking things at face value; forming and expressing opinions; making responsible decisions; exploring controversial issues and situations; examining the consequences of different actions; learning how to seek help and advice; reducing risk when working in the wider community	Participating in decision-making; working with others to campaign for change; taking part in debates and finding out more about local and global issues; using ICT or media such as film, drama and art to present and express ideas	Taking action on real issues and problems facing individuals and communities; working with others to try to influence, change or resist unwanted change; developing the knowledge, skills and confidence to participate effectively, responsibly and democratically; lobbying or campaigning on issues	Finding creative solutions to problems; expressing ideas and views effectively; negotiating; influencing others; learning about economic dimensions of political and social decisions; exploring the choices that governments have to make regarding taxation and public spending priorities

continued

	Be healthy	Stay safe	Enjoy and achieve	Make a positive contribution	Achieve economic well-being
Design and Technology	Understanding food hygiene; learning about the relationship between food, health, growth and energy balance; learning to prepare healthy food; investigating products to protect health	Following safe practices in the workshop; managing risk when using tools and equipment; thinking about the safety of others	Creating practical products in response to people's needs or wants; researching ideas and engaging with the world beyond school	Engaging in collaborative problem-solving activities; designing products that contribute positively to the community or environment	Generating practical cost-effective solutions that are relevant and fit for purpose; solving technical problems; responding creatively to briefs; developing proposals; working with designers; exploring career opportunities in design
English	Reading and writing for pleasure; exploring issues and expressing feelings through prose, poetry, drama and role play; reading to access health information	Developing the confidence to ask questions and express opinions; assessing the validity of opinions and information; exploring situations, dilemmas and relationships through texts, role play and drama	Experiencing the richness and breadth of literature; expressing ideas and opinions; creating new worlds in poetry and narrative; developing confidence through drama	Working collaboratively as part of a group discussion or drama activities; providing constructive responses to others' work; speaking, listening and writing for purposes beyond the classroom; contributing to school life through drama	Developing communication skills and literacy; expressing ideas and views effectively; exploring career opportunities in the creative and cultural industries
Geography	Investigating illness and disease around the world; comparing lifestyles in different countries	Developing safe working practices while carrying out fieldwork; exploring hazards and health risks in areas where people are not safe; questioning information and opinions and not taking things at face value	Learning about different environments, places, cultures and peoples; taking part in fieldwork; developing a sense of curiosity about the Earth	Considering their role as world citizens; learning about sustainable development; examining the social, environmental and economic impacts of what people do individually and collectively	Exploring how nations and peoples trade; researching, presenting and analysing information; appreciating the need for sustainable economic developments

Table 3.2 continued

	Be healthy	Stay safe	Enjoy and achieve	Make a positive contribution	Achieve economic well-being
History	Learning about personal and public health and their impact on life; exploring individual identity through personal and community history	Developing safe working practices while carrying out fieldwork and other investigations; exploring events in the past when people have not been safe; challenging information and being aware of bias and inaccuracies	Discovering rich and varied stories from the past; taking part in investigations and fieldwork; visiting museums, galleries and historical sites; connecting life today to life in the past	Learning about the lives of famous philanthropists; researching local history to find out who has helped to improve the community and how; learning how populations have pulled together in times of war	Exploring how working patterns and the nature of work have changed over time; challenging information and being aware of bias and inaccuracies; expressing ideas and views effectively; engaging in critical research
ICT	Accessing information on health and well-being; analysing nutritional data; using monitoring technology during exercise	Developing safe practice when using ICT (e.g. correct positioning of equipment and chairs, taking regular breaks); questioning information and not accepting it at face value; learning responsible use of email and the internet; avoiding disclosure of personal details	Using ICT to support creativity, initiative and independent thinking; conveying ideas in original ways; using ICT to work collaboratively; using ICT for music, film and photography	Accessing information and ideas on local, national and international issues; sharing information with people from diverse backgrounds; learning about equality of access, copyright and plagiarism; using forums	Learning when and how to use ICT skills to support work; developing ICT capability; obtaining, analysing and presenting information; using ICT to collaborate with others; learning how to manage finances online
Mathematics	Investigating numerical data related to health and diet; becoming financially capable and gaining greater control over factors affecting health	Understanding risk through the study of probability; making informed choices about investments, loans and gambling	Developing mathematical ways of perceiving the world; recognising underlying structures and connections between mathematical ideas; investigating games and strategies	Learning to use logic, data and generalisations with precision	Understanding and managing money; making sound economic decisions in daily life; learning about investments; reasoning with numbers; interpreting graphs and diagrams; communicating maths information

From: *Implementing the Every Child Matters Strategy*, Routledge © Rita Cheminais 2010

	Be healthy	Stay safe	Enjoy and achieve	Make a positive contribution	Achieve economic well-being
Modern Foreign Language	Building confidence through speaking another language; gaining a new perspective on the world and life in other countries	Communicating with strangers; dealing with unfamiliar situations in which communication is difficult; understanding others' customs and avoiding difficult or dangerous situations in travel	Extending horizons beyond this country; learning to communicate with people from different parts of the world; learning about different cultures and countries; gaining a sense of achievement from successful communication	Actively trying to understand and communicate with others; learning to be 'ambassadors' for their own country and culture	Learning to use business-related language; preparing to work in the international market
Music	Improving physical, mental and emotional well-being through singing, playing and listening to music	Developing critical skills and self-discipline; forming and expressing opinions about music	Gaining enjoyment from performing, composing and listening; taking part in musical activities and events; playing music with others	Contributing to school life as a performer, listener, organiser, music leader or in a supporting role	Working as part of a team to play or compose music; learning about the music industry
PE	Taking part in high-quality physical activity; developing a fitness programme; seeing physical activity as part of a lifelong healthy lifestyle; expressing emotions through dance; enjoying watching sport; learning about how the body works and why exercise and rest are important; exploring dietary habits	Learning the importance of following rules; taking part safely in outdoor and adventurous activities; minimising risk in physical activity	Participating and achieving as performers, officials and leaders; making links with physical activities, sport and dance in the community; taking part in creative, artistic, aesthetic, competitive and challenging activities; working as part of a team	Contributing to school life through sport; helping as an official, coach or administrator; contributing to a team performance; developing an understanding of fairness; working collaboratively on problem-solving challenges	Working individually and as part of a team; reviewing, refining and carrying out plans; learning about balancing work with leisure and social interaction; exploring career opportunities in sport

continued

Table 3.2 continued

	Be healthy	Stay safe	Enjoy and achieve	Make a positive contribution	Achieve economic well-being
PSHE	Learning about diet and healthy living; developing drug awareness; learning about sexual health; exploring self-identity and image; managing risk and dealing with social and moral dilemmas; withstanding peer pressure	Managing risk; developing safe working practices while engaged in work experience and enterprise activities; exploring personal, ethical and moral issues; developing first-aid skills; forming safe relationships; avoiding debt and financial hardship	Learning practical, real-life skills; taking part in enterprise activities; meeting new people	Working collaboratively on group activities; getting involved with the local community	Learning about progression routes into further education, employment and training; finding creative solutions to problems; learning to be adaptable; expressing ideas and views effectively; working well in groups; engaging in critical research; evaluating evidence; identifying and analysing different interpretations of issues and events; substantiating arguments and judgements
RE	Exploring morals and decision-making; learning about sexual health and ethics; exploring mediation and enlightenment; learning about spiritual rituals	Evaluating ideas, relationships and practices; learning about religious and ethical rules governing care of children, respect for friends and neighbours and responsibility for crime; learning about authority ethics, relationships and rights and responsibilities	Exploring and sharing beliefs, practices and feelings; engaging with issues of meaning and value; developing curiosity about religion in the modern world; searching for meaning; debating ideas; meeting people of different cultures and beliefs	Developing an appreciation of different points of view; investigating, discussing and building reasoned arguments; dealing with different beliefs respectfully; learning about justice, authority and interfaith dialogue; learning about faith groups in the community	Learning about religious and ethical rules surrounding the use of money; learning about equality, justice, prejudice, discrimination, human rights, fair trade, the environment and climate change; learning about religious issues in the workplace, such as diet, clothing, use of time for prayer, values and attitudes; learning about the work of charities; developing skills of listening, empathy and group collaboration

	Be healthy	Stay safe	Enjoy and achieve	Make a positive contribution	Achieve economic well-being
Science	Learning about diets, drugs, disease and contraception; understanding the consequences of poor diet and the misuse of alcohol and drugs	Following safe working practices in a laboratory; assessing and managing risk through scientific experiments; handling chemicals and biological materials safely; using electricity, heat and light safely	Developing curiosity about the world; carrying out practical investigations; exploring the effect of science on lives on a personal, local, national and global scale	Actively contributing to scientific investigations; learning about the relationship between science, society and the future of the world; considering ethical and moral issues; learning about global sustainability	Obtaining, analysing, evaluating and communicating data; engaging in critical research; exploring career opportunities in science

Source: *Every Child Matters at the Heart of the Curriculum* (2008) and reproduced here with permission of QCA. © Qualifications and Curriculum Authority 2008.

School-level indicators for pupil well-being

The prolonged and narrow focus on attainment for many years is considered to be an impediment to schools demonstrating their contributions to the wider ECM pupil well-being outcomes. In *21st Century Schools: A World-Class Education for Every Child*, the government acknowledged that:

> Schools are often unrecognised and unrewarded for improvements they make to children's lives, which do not show up in traditional attainment measures.
>
> (DCSF 2008b: 37)

The concept of developing strong school-level indicators to evaluate and measure the schools' contribution to promoting pupil well-being was first proposed in the government's Children's Plan, and is viewed as a way of addressing the balance between ECM and the standards debate. The indicators are a means of strengthening the school's accountability for pupil well-being, particularly in view of the school's statutory duty to promote the well-being of pupils.

The school-level indicators for pupil well-being feature in the revised Office for Standards in Education, Children's Services and Skills (OFSTED) inspection process, introduced in September 2009, and are used by inspectors as evidence to explore further the effectiveness of the school's contribution to well-being. They apply to all maintained schools, primary, secondary, special and pupil referral units, short stay schools, and to academies. The school-level indicators provide consistent, benchmarked data that, alongside other evidence, assist the school, OFSTED inspectors and the School Improvement Partner (SIP) to consider whether the data is being put to effective use by the school; how effectively the pupils' well-being is being promoted; and whether it could be promoted more effectively.

The Department for Children, Schools and Families (DCSF) and OFSTED acknowledge that schools should not be accountable for well-being outcomes over which they have limited influence – for example, the levels of child obesity or teenage pregnancy rates. Many of the indicators are 'proxy indicators' with an indirect relationship to ECM outcomes, and thus have inherent limitations that will not provide direct evidence on which to base or determine evaluative judgements. An over-reliance on what is quantifiable in relation to pupil well-being outcomes may devalue insightful analysis, particularly as many are 'soft' and are subjective data derived from OFSTED, parent, pupil, and staff perception surveys.

Six key principles in the use of school-level data on pupil well-being

The DCSF and OFSTED identified six key principles in relation to the use of pupil well-being indicators data, emphasising that:

- the school-level pupil well-being data should only be collected once and used many times by the school, local authority (LA), DCSF and OFSTED;
- use should be made of data and evidence already collected and available at school-level for pupil well-being;
- school-level data on pupil well-being should enable comparisons to be made between similar schools;
- the pupil well-being data at school-level must be useful to their own self-evaluation and improvement planning;
- the school-level pupil well-being data needs to be complemented by a profile of area-wide data on child well-being to put the school contribution into context, and to help inform provision from external agencies to enable the school to meet local needs;

- the school-level indicators for pupil well-being must relate to outcomes over which schools have a reasonable degree of influence.

During the initial consultation about these indicators, with headteachers via the NCSL, and teachers, through the General Teaching Council for England (GTC), each expressed a degree of concern about the reliability and validity of perceptions data, especially when it may be coloured and influenced by parents', staff or pupils' personal grudges or prejudices about negative isolated incidents relating to ECM and pupil well-being in the school. It is therefore important that the school supports these OFSTED surveys with other robust evidence that gives the context for why such a minority of negative views may be present in the OFSTED perception surveys.

Two types of school-level indicators for pupil well-being

Two kinds of school-level indicator are used:

1 Indicators from quantified outcomes over which schools have a significant and direct influence.
2 Indicators based on pupils', parents' and staff perceptions relating to the ECM outcomes and the school's contribution to them.

Both types of indicators will be complemented with a local-area well-being profile that comprises all the indicators in the National Indicator Set relevant to the well-being of children and young people, which gives national, regional and local benchmarks to support schools in their own self-evaluation of pupil well-being. The school-level indicators only provide a partial picture and a snapshot of pupil well-being and need to be used with care.

Quantitative school-level indicators for pupil well-being

The quantitative school-level indicators for pupil well-being include:

- the school's overall attendance rate for the most recent school year;
- the percentage of persistent absentees – pupils who have missed more than 20 per cent of sessions;
- the rate of permanent exclusions;
- the take-up of school lunches;
- the percentage of pupils doing at least two hours per week of PE and sport;
- post-16 progression measures, i.e. participation rates in learning in the year after pupils left compulsory schooling.

A school will want to add its own additional quantitative pupil well-being data, such as:

- the number of awards achieved by the school, e.g. Inclusion Quality Mark, Healthy Schools Status, Sports Mark, ECO-Schools, ECM Standards award;
- the take-up of extended services;
- engagement with other services;
- attendance rates for particular groups of pupils, e.g. special educational needs (SEN), looked after children (LAC) to identify any trends or patterns;
- the take-up of free school meals (FSM);
- the percentage of pupils eating healthy school meals or packed lunches;
- accessibility of PE and sport for different groups of pupils, e.g. those with SEN or disabilities, Muslim girls;
- diversity of pupils engaging with post-16 learning.

Qualitative school-level indicators based on ECM outcomes perceptions

Qualitative school-level indicators based on pupils', parents' and staff perceptions relating to the ECM outcomes and the school's contribution to them based on surveys ask the extent to which:

the school

- promotes healthy eating;
- promotes exercise and a healthy lifestyle or play for young children;
- discourages smoking, consumption of alcohol and use of illegal drugs and other harmful substances;
- gives good guidance on relationships and sexual health;
- helps pupils to manage their feelings and be resilient;
- promotes equality and counteracts discrimination;
- provides a good range of additional activities;
- gives pupils good opportunities to contribute to the local community;
- helps people of different backgrounds to get on well, both in school and in the wider community;
- helps pupils gain the knowledge and skills they will need in the future;
- offers the opportunity at 14 to access a range of curriculum choices;
- supports pupils to make choices that will help them progress towards a chosen career/ subject of further study.

pupils

- feel safe;
- experience bullying;
- know who to approach if they have a concern;
- enjoy school;
- are making good progress;
- feel listened to;
- are able to influence decisions in the school.

A school will wish to use a range of methods in addition to using the survey to gather the perceptions of pupils and parents. These may include:

- questionnaires
- school council
- pupil conferences
- house systems
- learning walks
- feedback from peer mentors
- forums
- weekly drop-in sessions
- focus groups
- circle time
- informal parent meetings
- pupil problem or suggestion boxes.

The school may utilise commercial data collection tools for pupil well-being, such as Pupil Attitudes to Self And School (PASS) or Measures of Children's Mental Health & Psychological Wellbeing: A Portfolio of Educational and Health Professionals, OFSTED Tell Us Survey, or, the Health Related Behaviour Questionnaire.

Tracking, recording and analysing pupils' progress in the ECM outcomes

In respect of standards and ECM complementing each other, schools need to give equal weight in their systems for tracking, recording and analysing quantitative and qualitative data relating to pupil attainment and well-being. This will result in schools updating existing systems in order to incorporate ECM outcomes information and data on tracking grids, pupil-level data capture spreadsheets and pupil reports for parents/carers.

Similarly, teachers and teaching assistants (TAs) will need to develop skills in recording, analysing and interpreting ECM outcomes pupil-level data, including reporting the impact of interventions and additional provision. Table 3.3 provides a model template of a suggested tracking grid for class and form teachers to utilise for recording pupils' progress in each of the five ECM outcomes. Ideally the class or form teacher would plot their classes' or forms' progress in relation to each of the five ECM well-being outcomes at the end of each term or every six months by putting the initials of pupils in the relevant boxes on the tracking grid.

Class and/or form teachers will need to gather evidence of pupils' progress in the five ECM outcomes from a range of children's workforce practitioners, not just from within school, but also from external agencies and other partners delivering extended services.

Tracking information helps to inform any necessary changes or modifications required to be made to additional provision or curriculum content. Tracking helps to:

- check pupils' progress towards meeting individual targets set for the ECM outcomes;
- keep a check on pupils' ongoing progress in relation to the additional provision and services put in place and being accessed;
- provide a vehicle for children's workforce practitioners to engage in a professional dialogue about pupils' progress in the five ECM outcomes;
- identify any pupils who may be underachieving on the ECM outcomes, or have gaps in their additional provision for well-being;
- highlight particular strengths or weaknesses existing in the coverage of the five ECM outcomes;
- inform any necessary revisions to ECM well-being pupil provision;
- demonstrate the value-added progress in the ECM outcomes;
- raise expectations about the importance of pupils' ECM well-being;
- contribute valuable evidence to the school's self-evaluation processes and to the OFSTED self-evaluation form (SEF), and the school-level indicators for pupil well-being;
- enable comparisons to be made with similar schools in relation to pupil progress on the five ECM outcomes.

Table 3.4 offers a second model template for tracking and recording individual pupil progress on the five ECM outcomes using a red, amber, green (RAG) rating system. This form of tracking and monitoring pupil progress for well-being will be useful for supporting external accountability requirements from the LA children's services, or specific agencies. It is particularly valuable for evidence gathered for the common assessment framework (CAF) or the team around the child (TAC) processes. The RAG system helps to flag up any concerns and alert other colleagues to a child's or young person's problems or difficulties as soon as possible in order that early intervention occurs. The class or form teacher complete the RAG and pass it on to the school's ECM manager to enable him or her to commission additional support, advice and interventions from the appropriate agencies.

Table 3.5 offers a more detailed qualitative recording system based on the CAF pre-assessment form. This form can be used for all pupils, as well as for those who may be at risk of achieving poor ECM well-being outcomes.

Table 3.3 Tracking the progress of a class on the five ECM outcomes

Class 6M	Be healthy	Stay safe	Enjoy and achieve	Make a positive contribution	Achieve economic well-being
Falling behind					
Stuck					
Reached expected progress					
Exceeded expected progress					

Place the initials of pupils in the respective ECM outcomes boxes, matched to the current level of progress.

From: *Implementing the Every Child Matters Strategy*, Routledge © Rita Cheminais 2010

Table 3.4 Tracking and recording individual pupil ECM outcomes

Name of pupil:			DOB:		Date of review:	
Be healthy	Red	Amber	Green	Evidence to support the RAG rating		Outcome measures
1						
2						
3						
4						
Stay safe	Red	Amber	Green	Evidence to support the RAG rating		Outcome measures
1						
2						
3						
4						
Enjoy and achieve	Red	Amber	Green	Evidence to support the RAG rating		Outcome measures
1						
2						
3						
4						
Make a positive contribution	Red	Amber	Green	Evidence to support the RAG rating		Outcome measures
1						
2						
3						
4						
Achieve economic well-being	Red	Amber	Green	Evidence to support the RAG rating		Outcome measures
1						
2						
3						
4						

Table 3.5 ECM outcomes qualitative recording form

Name of pupil: _____ Date of birth: _____ Form/Class: _____

ECM outcome/aspect	Yes	No	Not sure	Comments
Does the pupil appear to be healthy?				
Is the pupil safe from harm?				
Is the pupil enjoying school and achieving their optimum potential?				
Is the pupil making a positive contribution?				
Is the pupil developing the skills for achieving future economic well-being?				

Name of practitioner: _____ Job: _____

Date completed this pre-assessment checklist: _____

From: *Implementing the Every Child Matters Strategy*, Routledge © Rita Cheminais 2010

Engaging pupils in reviewing their own progress in the ECM outcomes

It is important that pupils not only set their own targets relating to the ECM outcomes, but that they also participate in reviewing their own progress. A good way to facilitate the pupil self-review process is with class or form teachers taking a lead role. A class day is devoted to reviewing pupils' progress in the five ECM outcomes. The day is set for the entire year group, from 8.30 a.m. to 6.30 p.m., which offers greater flexibility for parents and carers to attend, and alleviates those dreary long queues at the more traditional parents evenings. Multi-agency practitioners make themselves available to meet with parents/carers on the set day, where appropriate. The school's manager for ECM is also available on the respective day, circulating to each class or form in the particular year group to pick up any concerns and to answer any parental queries.

Each pupil is responsible for having completed their ECM log, which records the progress made towards meeting their ECM targets for the term. It also records any further help or future ECM targets the pupil requires. Those pupils who require support in completing their ECM log prior to the review day are allocated support from a TA who usually works with the class.

Figure 3.1 provides a model ECM log for pupil use. This can be customised or adapted to suit the age and ability of pupils. It is presented in a child-friendly format.

Disseminating good practice in the ECM outcomes

The manager of ECM in the school is responsible for disseminating good practice within the school. They need to ensure that they ask staff from within the school, those from multi-agencies and others from voluntary and community organisations who work with pupils, to provide examples of good practice which relate to improving either an individual, small group or a whole class's ECM outcome(s). It is useful if staff and other practitioner partners can provide these as short cameos or case studies, which are anonymous to protect the identity of individual children or young people. The manager of ECM can begin to compile an ECM portfolio of evidence, as a hard copy volume and in electronic format, to put on the school website, and to share in e-forums with other schools and the LA. Figure 3.2 provides a model template for recording good practice examples in the ECM outcomes.

Other formats for recording good practice examples in the ECM outcomes can be utilised. These include:

- photographic evidence;
- video recordings, podcasts or blogs;
- CD or DVD;
- media reports from the local or national press, including journal articles;
- school and official government websites;
- PowerPoint presentations via school cluster groups or learning networks;
- reports and briefings to staff, governors, parents, the school council and to the LA;
- school and LA newsletters;
- national e-forums, e.g. DCSF, DH, QCA, NCSL, TDA, GTC;
- the school's SEF;
- showcase events, e.g. ECM school, local or national conferences, roadshows, speed networking events, pupil summits, video diary room;
- small-scale school-based action research project accounts.

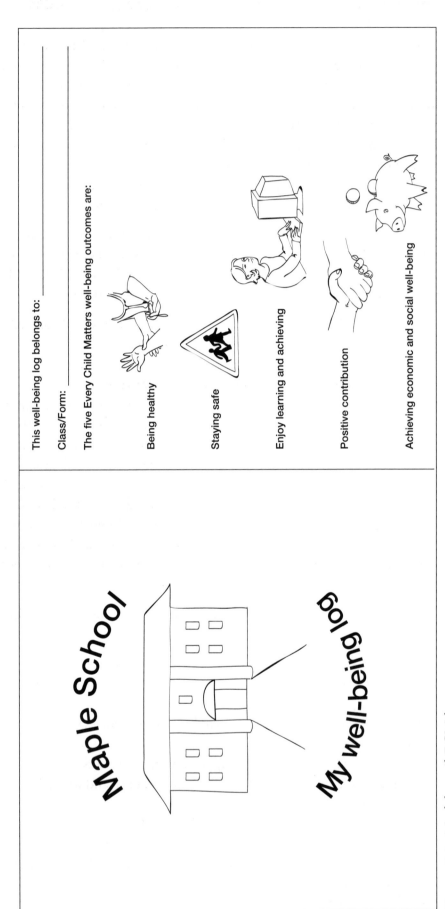

Figure 3.1 Model pupil ECM log

Being healthy

Put a ✓ in the relevant box/boxes

How do you keep healthy in school?

Exercise ☐   Eating and ☐   Keeping ☐   Managing ☐
PE, sport   drinking   hands   own
           healthily   clean   feelings

What else do you need to do to stay healthy in school?
_____

What do you do to have a healthy lifestyle outside school?
_____

Who can help you to stay healthy
(a) at school? _____
(b) at home? _____

What is your personal target for being healthy?
_____

How will you achieve this target?
_____

Being safe

Put a ✓ in the relevant box/boxes

How do you keep safe in school?

Report ☐   Learning and ☐   Keeping away ☐   Reporting any ☐
bullying   playing safely   from unsafe   strangers to
                                     areas   staff

Following school ☐   Looking after the ☐
fire drill   safety of others

What else do you need to do to keep safe in school?
_____

What do you do to keep safe outside school?
_____

Who can help you to stay even safer
(a) at school? _____
(b) at home? _____

What is your personal target for staying safe?
_____

How will you achieve this target?
_____

Figure 3.1 continued

Making a positive contribution

Put a ✔ in the relevant box/boxes

How do you make a positive contribution in school?

Expressing views to School Council ☐   Helping others ☐   Partaking in school events ☐   School prefect ☐

Study buddy ☐   Sensible citizen ☐   Form/class representative ☐   Partaking in after-school clubs ☐

What else do you need to do to make a positive contribution in school?
_____

What do you do to make a positive contribution at home and/or in the local community? _____
_____

Who can help you to make more of a positive contribution
(a) at school? _____
(b) at home/ in the community? _____

What is your personal target for making a positive contribution?
_____

How will you achieve this target?
_____

Enjoying learning and achieving

Put a ✔ in the relevant box/boxes

How do you enjoy learning and achieving in school?

Learning in a group or pair ☐   Using favourite learning style ☐   Presenting work in ways other than writing ☐   Valuing help of staff ☐

Enjoying going to school ☐   Liking learning new things ☐   Behaving sensibly ☐   Attending school clubs ☐

What else do you need to do to enjoy learning and achieve in school?
_____

What do you do to enjoy learning and to achieve outside school?
_____

Who can help you to learn and achieve
(a) at school? _____
(b) at home? _____

What is your personal target for enjoying learning and achieving?
_____

How will you achieve this target?
_____

Figure 3.1 continued

Self-review of the five well-being outcomes

Rate your overall progress in achieving the five well-being outcomes on a scale of 1–3
(1 = a little progress; 2 = average progress; 3 = good progress)

Being healthy ☐   Making a positive contribution ☐

Staying safe ☐   Achieving economic and social well-being ☐

Enjoying learning and achieving ☐

Which well-being outcome do you need to improve the most?

_____

What will you need to do to enable you to achieve this well-being outcome?

_____

Who can help you to achieve this well-being outcome
(a) at school? _____
(b) at home? _____

My overall main personal well-being target is:

_____

Date of self-review _____

Signature _____

Achieving economic and social well-being

Put a ✔ in the relevant box/boxes

How do you achieve economic and social well-being in school?

Team
working ☐

Making
sensible
decisions ☐

Looking for
new chances ☐

Managing
money ☐

Using ICT ☐

Ideas
about a
career ☐

Solving
problems ☐

What else do you need to do to achieve economic and social well-being in school?

_____

What do you do to achieve economic and social well-being outside school?

_____

Who can help you to achieve economic and social well-being
(a) at school? _____
(b) at home? _____

What is your personal target for achieving economic and social well-being?

_____

How will you achieve this target?

_____

Figure 3.1 continued

Title of the ECM activity	
Aims of the ECM activity	• • •
Timescale for the activity	
Target group of pupils	
Brief description of the ECM activity	
ECM outcomes covered by the project	
Impact of the activity on improving pupils' ECM well-being outcomes	• • •
Person leading the ECM activity	

Figure 3.2 ECM good-practice template

The following list of examples give some 'quick wins' and are easy to implement as part of everyday school ECM policy and practice.

- The school staff and governors' continuing professional development (CPD) programme is aligned to the five ECM outcomes.
- A school ECM team is formed as a developmental group, which includes representatives from school staff, multi-agency practitioners who work in the school, an ECM governor and an external partner from any voluntary or community organisations, or from the LA.
- The school council organises its meeting agendas by the ECM outcomes, and also links in to the school's ECM team.
- Curriculum schemes of work and lesson plans include and indicate coverage of the five ECM outcomes.
- The school works towards achieving an external award such as the national ECM Standards Award (www.ecm-solutions.org.uk), or the Healthy School Status (www.healthyschools.gov.uk) or Active Mark.
- Summer school and Easter school activities are planned around the ECM outcomes.
- The school prospectus links to and is aligned with the five ECM outcomes.
- The school website has an ECM webpage, or is aligned with and links to the five ECM outcomes.
- The school has an ECM calendar of events and activities.
- Pupils' portfolios of work are organised under the five ECM outcomes.
- School and classroom displays show their links to the five ECM outcomes.
- Reports to the governing body are organised and aligned with the five ECM outcomes.
- The governing body monitors the work of the school against the five ECM outcomes.
- There is one ECM governor or, preferably, five ECM governors – one for each of the five ECM outcomes.
- There are lead practitioners nominated for each one of the five ECM outcomes where the school is large enough, otherwise these staff, who may be teaching and non-teaching staff, working across a cluster of local schools.
- School assemblies are planned around the five ECM outcomes.
- The school has an ECM pupil charter.

The next five ECM good-practice examples are described in greater depth, and have largely arisen as a result of schools undertaking the national ECM Standards Award.

ECM cameo 1: pupils as ECM action researchers

(Although this activity was undertaken by one class in a school, five classes could each take a different ECM outcome).

The aims of the project were to:

- find out what the school was doing to ensure pupils were healthy, safe, enjoying and achieving, making a positive contribution and achieving economic well-being; and
- identify which ECM outcomes required further improvement.

A class of 30 pupils were divided up into five smaller groups by the class teacher. Each group researched one of the five ECM outcomes, and one pupil was nominated as the team leader responsible for reporting back on the findings from the group's research for the particular ECM outcome.

The class teacher and a member of the senior leadership team coached the class in the use and advantages of different research methods. The groups used observation, questionnaires, interviews and random sampling to gather evidence for the five ECM outcomes from other pupils in the school. The research field work took place over two weeks, using lunchtimes. Each group met together for one afternoon to discuss their findings on the following Monday afternoon, and to gather together their evidence for putting into a report and a PowerPoint presentation, which was to be shared with the senior leadership team, the governing body and the staff at a briefing session.

The class experienced: formulating the questions for interviews and questionnaires; conducting interviews; using a digital video camera; analysing qualitative and quantitative data; and presenting findings in a range of formats, using bar and pie charts, line graphs and written bullet-point lists. Six pupils from the class, which included each of the five team leaders and an overall pupil presenter, all contributed to writing and delivering the PowerPoint presentation to the various audiences.

The findings were used to inform the school improvement plan priorities and the class were given feedback by the headteacher on the next steps and actions that would be taken to address the issues identified from the research.

Although the project covered all five ECM outcomes it enabled pupils to:

- make a positive contribution
- enjoy and achieve.

ECM cameo 2: improving ECM in the local community

Six pupils from across the school's two key stages are nominated, via the school council, to work with the local community police constable and the local radio station to plan, script and broadcast a live radio call-in show for listeners to phone in, in response to the pupils' questions about how the local community could be made safer for children and young people.

The pupils devise the questions for listeners to the radio call-in show. These are discussed with the school's ECM manager, who accompanies the pupils to the local radio station. The pupils take it in turn to ask the questions during the live broadcast.

Listeners phone in and respond with ideas and suggestions to the pupils' questions. The pupils take back a recording of the broadcast and transcribe this, noting down the listeners' ideas and suggestions. The local police constable discusses with the pupils the order of priority for acting on the suggestions and ideas. The pupils are asked to identify what contributions they could make to putting some of the ideas into practice.

The pupils present their findings to the headteacher and the senior leadership team in school. The police constable is on hand to answer any queries from the team. The headteacher and the police constable identify sources of funding to carry out the first project suggested by the radio phone-in callers, which entails developing a pleasant garden area and play space for children and local residents to enjoy.

The community project work begins after the May half-term. A risk assessment is undertaken prior to the pupils going out into the community to work on making an area near the school a safer place to play. Health and safety rules and procedures are followed, and pupils work under the supervision of the community liaison worker and a member of staff from school. The results of the completed project are publicised in the local library and on the school website.

This project enabled the pupils involved to:

- make a positive contribution
- stay safe.

ECM cameo 3: annual pupil takeover day

This day takes place in November, in a school, to coincide with the Children's Commissioner in England's national takeover day, when nominated pupils undertake adult jobs for one day in schools across the country.

A number of adult jobs are advertised to all classes in a school in Key Stage 2, or if secondary phase, in Key Stage 3 and Key Stage 4. Interested pupils are invited to submit a written application to the headteacher, indicating why they would be suitable for the adult job applied for.

The headteacher, the ECM manager in the school, with a panel of governors, shortlist ten pupil applicants who are then interviewed by this panel. The seven successful pupils spend a day shadowing the adult whose role they will take on for a day. The annual takeover day usually takes place nationally in schools on 23 November.

The takeover day pupils took on adult roles in one school, which included: a school librarian; a site manager; a mid-day supervisor; a school cook; the headteacher; a school governor; and a school office administrator. The school undertook all the necessary risk assessments and followed the correct health and safety procedures.

At the end of the day, the pupils fed back to the adult whose role they had undertaken, indicating what they enjoyed most about the job and what they least liked. The pupils wrote a short report about their experience, which is included in their personal ECM pupil portfolio of evidence. Short accounts also appear on the school website.

This activity enabled the pupils involved to:

- make a positive contribution
- achieve economic well-being
- enjoy and achieve.

ECM cameo 4: ECM pupils video diary room

This activity takes place annually. It requires a film crew, which can be commissioned from a local secondary school, academy, college or from the LA. A film crew of two people should be sufficient – one to operate the video camera and the other to ask the pupils questions. At secondary-school level, sixth formers could undertake the filming and questioning. All the parents of the pupils being interviewed for the diary room were informed about the activity and were asked to give their written permission for their child to be filmed.

A room is set up in school, with a screen separating half the room from the pupil. Behind the screen there is the adult asking the pupil the questions, and the screen has a hole in the middle of it where the lens of the film camera points unobtrusively. The pupil being asked the questions about the ECM outcomes is unaware of the camera. The film crew usually gets through about 20 individual pupil film interviews in one day.

The pupils are nominated by their peers, and can be one from each class in a school, and they must represent each key stage within the school. Some suggested questions could include:

- What does the school do to make sure pupils are safe?
- What does the school do to help pupils to be healthy?
- What does the school do to make sure pupils enjoy school and achieve in their learning?
- What does the school do to enable pupils to help others in school or in the community?
- What does the school do to help pupils learn about the world of work?
- What else could the school do to make pupils feel safer at school?
- What more could the school do to improve pupils' health?
- What more could the school do to ensure pupils enjoy school and achieve their personal best?
- What more could the school do to make sure pupils can have a say and take part in school decision-making?
- What more could the school do to enable pupils to achieve economic well-being in the future?

Following the completion of filming session, the film is edited and then copied onto a CD. This is sent back to the school for viewing. The CD is played at a staff in-service education and training (INSET) day, and also shown to the governing body and the school leadership team. The CD presentation informs staff of the necessary improvements required in relation to the five ECM outcomes as identified by the pupils on the film.

This activity enabled the pupils involved in the video diary room to:

- make a positive contribution.

ECM cameo 5: annual pupil ECM showcase

A pupil committee in one school plan and organise the ECM school conference, which is an annual event to showcase the school's best practice in ECM. The pupil committee have a budget to manage, and within the confines of that they have to:

- commission a keynote speaker to open the conference;
- invite practitioners from the children's workforce from within school and from external agencies to deliver workshops;
- organise inputs from class groups or individual pupils to input throughout the day at the conference;
- commission caterers to provide refreshments during the day at the conference;
- find a suitable venue for the conference, with appropriate ICT facilities;
- produce publicity material to advertise the event to local schools and to the LA;
- agree upon an entrance ticket price to cover outgoing costs and to replenish funds in the conference budget;
- organise the printing of handouts and an evaluation form for the delegates conference packs.

The school ECM manager supports the work of the pupil conference planning committee, particularly in obtaining administrative support to handle the money and the invitations and replies from delegates attending the conference.

The event takes place on a day in July in the summer term. The local newspaper sends along a journalist to report on the conference. Significant moments from the conference are captured on film, and extracts are put onto the school's website.

Following the event, the pupil conference planning committee meet up with the ECM manager in school to discuss the feedback received from delegate evaluation sheets. They also evaluate whether the event was good value for money and identify the good practice in ECM that was shared during the day with the attending delegates.

This activity enabled the pupils planning and organising the showcase event to:

- meet all five ECM outcomes.

Questions for further reflection

1 What have been the most effective approaches to use in order to help school staff see the link between ECM and personalised learning?

2 As ECM manager, how have you ensured that the ECM outcomes are embedded consistently across the whole curriculum?

3 How have you ensured that qualitative school-level indicators for pupil well-being, based on perception surveys, are valid enough to feed into the SEF?

4 How have the school-level indicators for ECM pupil well-being been explained to parents and carers?

5 How have you evaluated the impact of ECM on pupils' achievements and progress?

6 From an analysis of the pupil-level ECM outcomes data, are there any groups of learners who are achieving poorly on some of the outcomes. If so, who are these pupils, and what will be done to address the issue?

7 How effective are the school's data systems for monitoring and tracking pupils' progress in the five ECM outcomes?

8 How best can the impact of ECM and its impact on pupil well-being be measured beyond the classroom?

9 What are the views of pupils telling you about the ECM outcomes in school?

10 What else could be done to engage the pupils more actively in reviewing their own progress on the ECM outcomes?

11 During the last 12 months, what have been the best examples of good or outstanding practice in ECM within the school?

4

Effective Partnerships for Delivering the Every Child Matters Outcomes

> **This chapter covers:**
> - building productive multi-agency partnerships for Every Child Matters (ECM);
> - strategies for engaging external partners in school improvement and self-evaluation processes for ECM;
> - working with parents and carers, other schools and the community to enhance ECM outcomes;
> - monitoring and evaluating the impact of partnerships for ECM;
> - the Children's Trust;
> - questions for further reflection.

Building productive multi-agency partnerships for ECM

Partnership entails a group of professionals joining together to collectively take responsibility for intervening early in order to remove barriers to learning and to improve children's and young people's ECM well-being outcomes. Different agencies working together in schools with extended services help to break down any traditional professional and cultural barriers, thus promoting more effective partnerships.

Depending on the school's context and the complexity of its pupil population, there can be anything from 25 up to 150 different external agencies engaging with the education setting. The manager of ECM in the school plays a crucial role in building productive multi-agency partnerships, along with other middle managers such as the Extended School Co-ordinator, the Special Educational Needs Coordinator (SENCO), and the Child Protection Officer. Coordinating multi-agency provision for pupils within the school can be extremely time consuming and complex. Getting to grips with partnership working right from the start is essential in order to remove any potential barriers that may hinder effective multi-agency working. The following checklist for planning and developing partnership working provides a useful point of reference for the school's ECM manager.

> **Checklist for productive partnership working**
> - The aims, goals and key purpose of the partnership are clear.
> - It is clear what all multi-agency practitioners bring to the partnership.
> - Realistic expectations exist as to what the multi-agency partnership can hope to achieve in the allocated timescale.
> - Careful consideration has been given to multi-agency partners' diversity, culture and sensitivities.
> - Realistic targets, objectives and milestones have been set for the multi-agency partnership.
> - Respective responsibilities of members of the multi-agency partnership are clear.
> - A 'no-blame' culture exists if outcomes from the partnership are not as successful as first envisaged.

Productive partnerships between the school and external agencies are reliant on joint working relationships being based on trust, mutual respect, information sharing, agreed objectives, clarity of roles, collective responsibility and ownership for improving children's and young people's ECM well-being outcomes. Processes such as the common assessment framework (CAF), the lead professional and the team around the child (TAC) are designed to promote collaborative partnership working.

The Office for Standards in Education, Children's Services and Skills (OFSTED) and Sure Start identified key features of effective multi-agency partnership working. In summary these are:

- Holding multi-disciplinary team meetings every week or half-term in the school to raise any concerns, review progress and share ideas and good practice.
- Establishing a communal multi-disciplinary working area/base with access to ICT, telephones and administrative support.
- Having a designated senior member of the school staff who oversees and coordinates multi-agency partnerships, and who acts as a point of contact for external practitioners.
- Providing a good-quality induction programme for any new multi-agency practitioners joining the school.
- Offering work-shadowing opportunities and cross-service working to help multi-agency practitioners to understand each others' roles.
- Providing continuing inter-professional learning and joint training opportunities within the school.
- Promoting networking to enable multi-agency practitioners to showcase and disseminate their good practice in partnership working.
- Establishing a web page or link on the school's website for multi-agency partnership working in order to publicise and promote such work.
- Involving external multi-agency professionals in school improvement planning and school self-evaluation processes, including inviting them to become representatives on the governing body and/or on the senior leadership team.
- Having in place a multi-agency partnership agreement, policy and mission statement.
- Undertaking joint monitoring and evaluation of multi-agency partnerships and collaborative working, which feeds into the school's self-evaluation form (SEF).

School leaders and managers of ECM are likely to have a hybrid of multi-agency team members, some who are familiar with the school's ways of working, and others who are new external practitioners working with pupils in the school. Developing and building a united multi-disciplinary school team requires careful human resource management at a strategic and operational level. The Department for Children, Schools and Families (DCSF) published the findings from workshops on the children's workforce in December 2008, and in relation to the effectiveness of multi-disciplinary/cross-professional working it found:

> It's almost irrelevant what service you offer or how good your service is, if there isn't a relationship there with the other partners then you're four steps back before you start.
>
> (DCSF 2008: 6)

The report goes on to add:

> Where you've got a relationship between five or six people because they work together, the speed at which they get to where they need to be is impressive, and their ability to get a response is improved.
>
> (DCSF 2008: 7)

Figures 4.1, 4.2 and 4.3 provide some suggested activities that help to clarify multi-agency practitioners' roles, knowledge, skills and collective contributions in working collaboratively within a school or other similar education setting.

The National College for Leadership of Schools and Children's Services (NCLSCS) offer a couple of useful publications to support the development of multi-agency partnership working. These are the Multi-Agency Team Toolkit and Every Child Matters (ECM) The Best of ECM Leadership Direct. The publications can be downloaded from the NCSL website: http://lmscontent.ncsl.org.uk/ECM.

The activities described in Figures 4.1, 4.2 and 4.3 are useful to undertake in September, and to revisit again at the end of the school's academic year, alongside external partners.

It is also recommended that the ECM manager in the school collects good-practice multi-agency partnership working case studies and cameos and compiles a portfolio of evidence to exemplify successful outcomes. Schools and services can also strengthen their partnership working by engaging with the national Multi-Agency Partnership Award, which acknowledges and rewards good and outstanding practice in nine aspects of partnership work. Further information about this award is available at www.ecm-solutions.org.uk.

Strategies for engaging external partners in school improvement and self-evaluation processes for ECM

Several schools are already encouraging multi-agency professionals who work with pupils in their setting to be representatives on the governing body and/or on the senior leadership team.

The following recommended strategies for engaging external multi-agency partners in the school's improvement planning and self-evaluation processes are approaches that readily embed into existing school practice, and which create little – if any – extra work.

The multi-agency partnership school improvement day

An annual multi-agency partnership school improvement day is held during the beginning of the summer term in the school. Multi-agency practitioners meet together as a team with the senior leadership team within the school to discuss the multi-disciplinary team's contributions to meeting the current school improvement priorities for ECM. The day concludes with the multi-agency practitioners identifying the activities and actions they will take in order to meet the new ECM school improvement priorities for the forthcoming academic year. Multi-agency practitioners may find the form illustrated in Figure 4.4 helpful in recording their contributions to the current and future school improvement priorities. The senior leadership team are responsible for ensuring that school staff know which priorities the multi-agency team will be contributing to during the next academic year.

Multi-agency practitioners school self-evaluation day

Multi-agency practitioners are invited to have individual meetings with the ECM manager in the school to discuss the impact of their work and how it will feed back anonymously into the OFSTED school SEF. Individual meetings usually take 30–45 minutes, and multi-agency practitioners find it helpful to have completed the relevant SEF sections prior to this meeting. Figure 4.5 provides an example of an SEF recording sheet for multi-agency practitioners to use. Depending on the role of the external practitioner, not all sections will be completed. This one-to-one meeting with the school's manager of ECM does not form part of any appraisal or performance management review, as that is the role of the service manager. However, multi-

Name: _____ **Service:** _____

Position: _____ **Timescale:** _____

Key roles	ECM outcomes
1	
2	
3	
4	
5	

Impact of interventions and support	Success measures
1	
2	
3	
4	
5	

Additional comment:
(Any specific requirements to improve your working arrangements/service delivery)

Figure 4.1 Model framework for identifying multi-agency roles and impact

From: *Implementing the Every Child Matters Strategy*, Routledge © Rita Cheminais 2010

Name: _____   **Service:** _____

Position: _____   **Date:** _____

What I bring to the multi-agency partnership		
Knowledge	**Skills**	**Experience**

The most significant contribution I have made to multi-agency team working this year in school:

_____

_____

_____

_____

_____

_____

_____

_____

_____

The aspects of multi-agency partnership working I would welcome further training in are:

_____

_____

_____

_____

Figure 4.2 Model template for identifying the knowledge, skills, experience and contributions of multi-agency practitioners

From: *Implementing the Every Child Matters Strategy*, Routledge © Rita Cheminais 2010

Multi-Agency Team Task

Together, as members of the school's multi-agency team, discuss the following statements relating to the features of partnership working.

Identify five of the most important features of partnership working, and list them in order of priority.

Give a reason for choosing each of the five features selected.

Use these five features as a point of reference for partnership working in school.

Overall, agree the single most important feature for multi-agency partnership working.

MULTI-AGENCY PARTNERSHIP WORKING STATEMENTS

1 Listening to the views of other practitioners in the team.
2 Valuing and acknowledging the contributions of other team practitioners.
3 Participating in joint collaborative decision-making.
4 Being respected by other team members.
5 Participating in inter-professional training and development activities.
6 Taking collective ownership and responsibility for removing barriers to children and young people's learning and well-being.
7 Finding solutions to problems in partnership with others.
8 Sharing ideas, knowledge, skills, expertise and experience with other team members.
9 Being able to effect change within the school.
10 Having a multi-agency partnership agreement.
11 Having a clear understanding about each others' roles and responsibilities.
12 Having effective two-way communication across partner agencies.

Figure 4.3 Team-building activity to strengthen multi-agency partnerships

From: *Implementing the Every Child Matters Strategy*, Routledge © Rita Cheminais 2010

Name: _____ **Service:** _____

Timescale: _____

School improvement plan priorities	Activities contributing to priorities
1	1
2	2
3	3

Further comments relating to individual contributions to current priorities:

Suggested future school improvement priorities for ECM/pupil well-being:

Contributions I could make to these suggested future priorities:

Figure 4.4 Recording multi-agency contributions to school improvement

Photocopiable Resource

Name: ______________________ **Service:** ______________________

Date of evaluation completion: ______________________

What impact have your contributions had on enabling pupils to enjoy and achieve?

To what extent have your interventions enabled pupils to feel safe?

To what extent have your interventions enabled pupils to adopt a healthy lifestyle?

To what extent have your interventions enabled pupils to contribute to the school and to the wider community?

To what extent have your interventions helped pupils to develop skills for future economic well-being?

Figure 4.5 Multi-agency practitioners record for school SEF evidence

agency practitioners may wish to make reference to this SEF evidence recording sheet during any formal performance management review with their service line manager.

Multi-agency schools networking event/conference

This day may be organised as a school cluster group activity, or as a whole local authority (LA) event. The purpose and focus of the event is to celebrate and share good practice in multi-agency partnership working across schools. The planning group for the event will need to incorporate a range of presentations, workshops, speed networking, and 'real' stories that illustrate the impact in improving ECM outcomes for children and young people. Multi-agency practitioners from across the different services, as well as private, voluntary and community sector partners who have made significant contributions to pupil well-being will be invited to deliver inputs at the event, as well as children, young people and their families.

Those attending the conference from schools will be headteachers, the ECM governor, the ECM manager, LA officers, the elected council member for children's services, and any other external experts in the field of pupil well-being and ECM.

Working with parents/carers and the community on ECM

Parents have a natural link with the community. Combining ECM activities for parents and community members is a good idea. A parent-to-parent approach is less daunting for community members, which often encourages wider participation, empowerment and engagement with the school. There are a range of methods for engaging parents and community members in the school's ECM agenda. These include:

- introducing a calendar of school ECM events for parents and the community;
- running parent workshops planned and organised around the five ECM outcomes;
- operating a password-protected ECM internet buddy scheme for parents;
- producing an ECM community and parent newsletter which provides progress updates on school ECM developments, as well as publicising events and activities for ECM;
- holding an annual parent/community ECM summit/conference which celebrates the school's work in improving children's well-being.

The aim and purpose of targeting ECM activities and events at parents and members of the local community is to help bridge the gap between home and school, as well as creating a greater understanding of the culture reflected in the locality. The school's ECM manager will need to act as the main facilitator of parent/community ECM networking events and activities.

Parent/community ECM action team

The school's ECM manager will invite interested parents and community members to form a parent-led action team, focused on developing an aspect of ECM from a parent/community perspective. The action team will agree upon an ECM project, identify necessary resources, allocate tasks to various members of the team, and plan for when the project will be monitored, evaluated and the outcomes celebrated. Examples of the type of ECM projects a parent/community action team may engage with are:

- setting up a parent helpline to respond to their ECM outcomes enquiries;
- holding a healthy-eating cookery competition for parents;

- introducing a school-based parent award scheme for supporting their child's well-being at home;
- establishing a tranquillity garden area in the school grounds for parents and children to utilise.

ECM parent/community café activity

This is a good way of engaging a larger number of parents and local community members in productive discussions about ECM issues that are of interest to all of them. The workshop would be facilitated by the ECM manager in school. This activity can be held after school in the early evening, between 6 p.m. and 8 p.m.

A series of five tables which each seat five parents/community members, set out in bistro/café style, with table cloths, need to be set out in the school hall, with tea, coffee, hot chocolate and pastries being available throughout the evening. Each table focuses on one of the five ECM outcomes. The table nominate a host who stays at the table, while others move round to the other four tables.

Flip-chart paper, 'post-it' notes and marker pens will be available on each table. The ECM manager will set an initial question relating to their respective ECM outcome for each table. Discussion will take place for 20 minutes on each table, and one person will record the main points arising from the table discussion on flip-chart paper. After 20 minutes everyone at the table apart from the host moves on to a different ECM outcome table. Another 20-minute discussion takes place, and any different points are added to the flip-chart paper. The process is repeated until all five ECM outcome tables have been circulated around.

The ECM manager as facilitator displays the flip charts with points from each table on the wall of the dining room, and everyone has ten minutes to view the comments. Following the event, a PowerPoint presentation is produced by the ECM manager, which records the outcomes from the café activity. This is placed on the school website, and highlights are also publicised in the school newsletter to parents. These comments inform the school improvement plan.

Monitoring and evaluating the impact of partnerships for ECM

The effectiveness and impact of multi-agency working in schools is dependent on the quality, strength and sustainability of the collaborative partnerships existing between services and the education setting. The manager of ECM will find the following checklist helpful for monitoring and evaluating multi-agency partnership working in school.

Checklist for monitoring and evaluating multi-agency partnerships
- There are clear plans and procedures in place for monitoring and evaluating multi-agency partnerships.
- Everyone involved understands the monitoring and evaluation processes being used.
- Monitoring and evaluation of multi-agency partnerships is robust and systematically undertaken by the school.
- There is a named person in school responsible for monitoring and evaluating the impact and outcomes of multi-agency partnership working.
- Clear, agreed shared objectives are used for monitoring and evaluating multi-agency partnership working.
- An external critical friend offers an objective perspective to the process.
- Everyone is clear that the effectiveness of the partnership in addition to the impact and outcomes of multi-agency working are being monitored and evaluated.
- All relevant key stakeholders are involved in the evaluation process.
- There is an agreed and known timescale for reporting back on multi-agency partnership working.
- Information on the impact and outcomes of multi-agency partnership working is reported back in accessible formats for a range of different audiences.

The Children's Trust

It is important that the headteacher and the manager of ECM have a clear understanding about the role and functions of the local Children's Trust, particularly as maintained schools, academies, sixth form and further education (FE) colleges are key partners of it.

A Children's Trust is a local area partnership led by the LA, which brings together public, private, community and voluntary sector organisations responsible for services for children, young people and families in order to:

- improve their well-being as defined by the five ECM outcomes through early intervention and prevention;
- improve their future prospects by narrowing the gap on educational attainment between vulnerable children and their peers;
- redress inequalities between the most disadvantaged children and their peers by reducing child poverty.

A Children's Trust achieves the above by:

- listening to the views of children, young people and families in order to identify the type of services to deliver to meet their needs;
- promoting joint working between professionals across different services;
- ensuring effective commissioning (i.e. planning and delivery) of services for children, young people and families through the flexible use of resources, e.g. pooling budgets;
- addressing any gaps existing in provision in order to respond to unmet needs, which may include delivering children's workforce training to help build capacity;
- overcoming any barriers to sharing and using information across services, e.g. CAF, ContactPoint.

The Children's Trust enables schools and other education settings to get the support they need in order to help them deliver their duty to promote pupil well-being. The Children's Trust, as a planning body, informs the commissioning decisions which ensure that front-line services work together to improve outcomes. For example, where a multi-agency team works through a local Sure Start children's centre or within a full-service extended school. In addition to commissioning services, the Children's Trust may also provide some services.

Commissioning services

The Children's Trust commissions services for children, young people and their families. This process entails:

* undertaking a joint strategic needs assessment to find out what services are required;
* planning and assessing which services are best placed to deliver in order to meet the identified needs;
* assessing the effectiveness and monitoring the impact of the services provided.

Commissioning usually operates at three different levels within the Children's Trust system:

1 Strategic – whole-service commissioning for a local area including regional collaboration for specialist services.
2 Operational or local – commissioning for school clusters, or through multi-agency teams operating in a locality.
3 Individual – through a lead professional commissioning individualised packages of support.

Extended schools, academies and colleges will also be commissioning services themselves, usually in collaboration with other schools and community partners. They use their own pooled budgets and expertise to procure services to meet the needs of not only their own pupils and students, but those of other children and young people in the local area. Some of these universal services may be co-located and integrated on or near the school site, or within a children's centre. Further information about Children's Trusts, and commissioning services is available on the government's ECM website at www.dcsf.gov.uk/everychildmatters/about/aims/childrenstrusts/childrenstrusts.

Questions for further reflection

1 How is the school making best use of its partnerships with external agencies to promote and improve the ECM outcomes?
2 What is working well in partnership working with other agencies?
3 What aspects of collaborative partnership working require further attention and development?
4 What does the school and its external partners need to do differently in order to improve the delivery of the ECM outcomes for children and young people?
5 Which factors are enabling the multi-agency team to work effectively in the school?
6 What does good multi-agency partnership working look like in the school?
7 How well does the school work in partnership with others to promote pupil well-being?
8 What are the views of service users telling you about the school's multi-agency partnerships?
9 What are multi-agency service providers telling you about the effectiveness and impact of partnership working in the school?
10 What have been the most effective approaches for sustaining productive partnerships with external agencies?
11 How are decisions that involve external partners taken, and how do these relate to the use of the CAF, working with other agencies, TAC and any identified lead professionals outside the school?
12 How far can the impact of multi-agency provision in school be contributed to the quality of the collaborative partnerships existing between the different agencies?
13 How will closer partnership working be established with any new or potential future partners providing services to improve pupil well-being?

Meeting the OFSTED Inspection Requirements for Every Child Matters

> **This chapter covers:**
>
> - collecting Every Child Matters (ECM) evidence for the Office for Standards in Education, Children's Services and Skills (OFSTED) self-evaluation form (SEF);
> - observing the ECM outcomes in the classroom;
> - inspection questions on ECM for school leaders and the ECM manager;
> - OFSTED surveys for key stakeholders on the ECM outcomes;
> - questions for further reflection.

Collecting ECM evidence for the OFSTED SEF

Section A of the streamlined OFSTED SEF, introduced in September 2009, aims to capture the school's evaluation of its work. The SEF is:

- clearer and simpler to understand;
- less time consuming to complete;
- shorter, providing a more strongly evaluative summary;
- a more effective evaluation tool to inform school improvement.

The electronic SEF structure matches that of the inspection schedule of judgements. When completing the SEF it is important to refer to the OFSTED grade descriptors and associated guidance provided by OFSTED, which is available to download from their website, by clicking on the tab entitled *forms and guidance*. This will help school leaders, the ECM manager and other staff to make accurate evaluations about aspects of the school's work, and in particular about the five ECM outcomes.

The SEF helps schools to systematically evaluate the contribution they and other partners are making towards delivering the five ECM outcomes. It is important to remember that the SEF provides inspectors and other external professionals such as the school improvement partner (SIP), with the first source of evidence on the way the school gathers and responds to the five ECM pupil well-being outcomes.

The SEF asks the following questions in relation to the five ECM outcomes:

- How well do pupils achieve and enjoy their learning?
- To what extent do pupils feel safe?
- To what extent do pupils adopt healthy lifestyles?
- To what extent do pupils contribute to the school and wider community?

- How well do pupils develop workplace and other skills that will contribute to their future economic well-being?

There are other SEF aspects that relate to pupils well-being outcomes:

- pupil behaviour;
- pupil attendance;
- the extent of pupils' spiritual, moral, social and cultural development (SMSC);
- the effectiveness of care, guidance and support;
- the effectiveness of partnerships in promoting learning and well-being;
- the effectiveness of safeguarding procedures.

Before exemplifying the OFSTED grade descriptors for the five ECM outcomes in more detail, it is useful to describe what ECM provision/outcomes should look like in a good-quality evaluative SEF.

ECM provision/outcomes in a school should demonstrate:
- Good and improving success rates in the five ECM outcomes.
- Significant improvements in ECM outcome trends over a three-year period.
- Well-established, inclusive, robust and accurate self-evaluation of the ECM outcomes.
- Rigorous procedures for ECM target-setting, monitoring and action planning.
- Good value for money in relation to the effectiveness and impact of external partnerships the school has in order to promote and deliver the ECM outcomes.
- Effective staff deployment and professional development that has a positive impact on improving pupils' ECM well-being outcomes.
- Significant improvements in organisational performance across the five ECM outcomes.

Table 5.1 illustrates the OFSTED grade descriptors for the five ECM outcomes.

Observing the ECM outcomes in the classroom

The OFSTED inspection process enables the headteacher or a member of the senior leadership team to undertake joint lesson observations with the OFSTED lead inspector. This is clearly advantageous because it enables a professional dialogue about the quality, effectiveness and impact of classroom practice on pupils' learning and their wider well-being to take place in partnership. An experienced OFSTED inspector also helps to validate the accuracy of the school leaders' judgements relating to classroom practice.

Following a joint lesson observation, the lead inspector will ask the headteacher or the senior leadership team member for their views about the strengths of the lesson, what would make the lesson better, and how good the lesson was overall. The inspector will then offer their own view of the lesson quality and explore any differences in judgements. The inspector will provide brief feedback to the teacher following the lesson observation.

The focus of lesson observations during the inspection are usually based on issues identified in the OFSTED lead inspector's pre-inspection brief, and/or from early inspection activity in the school.

In relation to observing the ECM outcomes in lessons, Figure 5.1 provides a template for headteachers and the ECM managers to use in school.

The headteacher and/or the ECM manager will find it useful to refer to the OFSTED grade descriptors for the five ECM outcomes to support their judgements during a lesson observation (as illustrated in Table 5.1). Attaching a copy of the actual grade descriptors for each of the ECM

Table 5.1 Descriptors for the five ECM outcomes based on OFSTED grades

ECM outcomes	Outstanding (1)	Good (2)	Satisfactory (3)	Inadequate (4)
Be healthy – the extent to which pupils adopt healthy lifestyles	Almost all groups of pupils have a great deal of knowledge and understanding of the factors affecting many aspects of their physical and mental health and emotional well-being. Many pupils adopt healthy lifestyles. Many groups of pupils, including those at risk, are keen to take action to improve their health and take up activities to do so with enthusiasm. A wide range of pupils respond positively to the school's health promotion strategies and are ambassadors for health promotion when talking to others.	Pupils know and understand many of the important factors which affect the different aspects of their health. Most want to take action to improve their health and participate regularly in activities which enable them to do so. A majority of pupils have adopted a healthy lifestyle. Pupils respond well to the school's health promotion strategies and may be involved in running health-related activities.	Pupils understand the main threats to their health and how they can be avoided. Some, although not the majority of pupils, want to take action to improve their health and do so through activities provided by school. Pupils are generally interested in the school's health promotion strategies.	A considerable number of pupils are unaware of factors affecting their health and express no wish to improve their knowledge. Few pupils have taken effective action to improve their health.
Stay safe – the extent to which pupils feel safe	Pupils have an excellent understanding about what constitutes unsafe situations. They maintain a well-tuned perspective on their own safety and that of others. Pupils say they feel safe at school at all times. Groups representing a wide range of pupils are entirely confident that issues they raise will be dealt with promptly and effectively by the school.	Different groups of pupils say they feel safe at school. Pupils generally understand what constitutes an unsafe situation. Pupils have an accurate perspective on their own safety and that of others. Pupils are confident that issues they raise will be dealt with promptly and effectively by the school.	Pupils say they usually feel safe at school. Pupils know about the main risks they might face and understand how these risks may threaten their own and others' safety. Pupils are clear that issues they raise will be taken seriously by the school and appropriate action taken.	Pupils, or a significant group, who understand what constitutes an unsafe situation at school say they do not feel safe. Pupils have a worryingly inaccurate perspective on their own safety. Pupils have little confidence in the school's ability to deal with safety issues.

From: *Implementing the Every Child Matters Strategy*, Routledge © Rita Cheminais 2010

continued

ECM outcomes	Outstanding (1)	Good (2)	Satisfactory (3)	Inadequate (4)
Enjoy and achieve – how well pupils achieve and enjoy their learning	The pupils acquire knowledge, develop understanding and learn and practise skills exceptionally well. Pupils demonstrate excellent concentration and are rarely off-task, even in extended periods without direction from an adult. They have developed resilience when tackling challenging activities in a range of subjects. Their keenness and commitment to succeed in all aspects of school life and ability to grasp opportunities to extend and improve their learning are exceptional. Progress is at least good in each key stage, key subjects and for different groups and is exemplary in some.	The pupils acquire knowledge, develop understanding and learn and practise skills well. The pupils are keen to do well, apply themselves diligently in lessons and work at a good pace. The pupils seek to produce their best work and are usually interested and enthusiastic about their learning in a range of subjects. A very large majority of groups of pupils make at least good progress and some may make outstanding progress, with nothing that is inadequate.	The extent to which pupils acquire knowledge, develop understanding and learn and practise skills is at least satisfactory. Most pupils work effectively in a range of subjects when provided with appropriate tasks and guidance but lack confidence in improving the quality of their work. Pupils generally work steadily and occasionally show high levels of enthusiasm and interest. The pupils make the progress expected given their starting point and some, although not the majority, may make good progress. Progress is inadequate in no major respect (for example, a key stage or particular groups of pupils), and may be good in some respects.	The extent to which pupils acquire knowledge, develop understanding and learn and practise skills is inadequate. Too many pupils fail to work effectively unless closely directed by an adult and give up easily. Pupils do not enjoy the activities provided, which is reflected in poor completion of tasks across a range of subjects. Pupils, or particular groups of pupils, make too little progress in one or more key stages.
Make a positive contribution – the extent to which pupils contribute to the school and the wider community	Pupils are very proud of and committed to their school community. This is demonstrated by their enthusiastic promotion of a broad range of activities to improve the school and the wider community. Most groups of pupils are represented in taking on responsibilities. Pupils from a wide range of groups have a strong voice in decisions relating to their learning and well-being. The pupils' involvement in the school and their interaction in the wider community are substantial and highly valued.	Pupils value their school community and willingly take on responsibility and participate constructively in school life beyond routine lessons and activities. Pupils hold clear views about their learning and well-being and participate keenly in discussions about these matters. Pupils understand and care about the issues facing their local area and, where appropriate, suggest and take actions to help improve the school and wider community. Pupils' behaviour in the local area is well regarded.	Pupils take on responsibility and play a constructive role in the school. Pupils have some influence on decisions about school life. Pupils support initiatives to improve aspects of life in school and the wider community. Pupils' behaviour promotes a positive relationship with the school's local community.	Pupils generally are reluctant to take on responsibilities or to play a part in the life of the school and wider community. Pupils have little or no influence on decisions which affect the quality of their learning and well-being. Pupils' contribution to the school and wider community has little positive impact.

Table 5.1 continued

ECM outcomes	Outstanding (1)	Good (2)	Satisfactory (3)	Inadequate (4)
Achieve economic well-being – the extent to which pupils develop workplace and other skills that will contribute to their future economic well-being	The pupils' application of their basic skills across many areas of school life is innovative and highly effective. Pupils have a wide range of well-honed skills that are highly relevant to the next phase of their life in education, training, employment or other constructive activity. Pupils are aspirational, know precisely what they need to do and are determined to succeed. Pupils' attendance is above average and punctuality is exemplary.	The pupils successfully apply their well-developed basic skills for a broad range of purposes and are well equipped with wider skills and personal qualities. Pupils have a good understanding of the next steps they need to take, and intend to take, to succeed in the future. Pupils' attendance is at least average and they are consistently punctual.	The pupils apply their basic skills securely in a range of contexts. Pupils develop the wider skills and personal qualities needed to equip them for the next phase of their education or the world of work and training. Pupils recognise the next steps they will need to take to achieve their goals. Pupils' attendance is generally average and they are usually punctual. In exceptional circumstances attendance may be low but is rapidly improving.	Application of basic skills is weak. A significant minority of pupils are not developing the knowledge, skills and understanding needed to succeed in the next phase of their lives. Pupils' attendance and punctuality generally, or for a significant minority, are poor and show no sign of improvement.

Source: From the evaluation schedule of judgements for schools inspected under section five of the Education Act 2005, from September 2009, Ofsted 2009 © Crown Copyright, reproduced here with permission.

LESSON OBSERVATION EVIDENCE FORM

Observer:		Date:		Observation time:

Class/Year:		Subject:		Teacher:		TA(s)

Focus	Context

Evaluation

Summary of main points (i.e. strengths and areas for further development)

Judgement on overall lesson quality in relation to pupils well-being

1 = Outstanding; 2 = Good; 3 = Satisfactory; 4 = Inadequate

Be healthy	Stay safe	Enjoy and achieve	Make a positive contribution	Achieve economic well-being	Care, guidance and support	Behaviour

Particular evaluations related to SMSC, partnerships in promoting learning and well-being (e.g. extended services)

Figure 5.1 Template for recording ECM outcomes evidence in lessons

From: *Implementing the Every Child Matters Strategy*, Routledge © Rita Cheminais 2010

outcomes – which highlights whether the teacher's current practice is outstanding, good, satisfactory or inadequate – with the written record of the lesson observation can help the teacher to know which particular aspects of an ECM outcome they need to focus on for further improvement.

Inspection questions on ECM for school leaders and the ECM manager

During inspection OFSTED will explore how the school has used the information gathered from the pupil, parent and any staff surveys, the quantitative indicators and other school sources to inform their self-evaluation of the ECM outcomes. The school-level indicators help schools to analyse and assess how well they are promoting the well-being of their pupils; their strengths, weaknesses and impact of the school's contribution to improving pupils' well-being in partnership with others, and where the school could improve its contribution to the ECM outcomes for its pupils.

The school leader and manager of ECM in the school will find the following questions useful when evaluating and reviewing the school-level indicators for pupil well-being.

- Are there any particular groups of pupils or individual pupils who are achieving poorly in a particular ECM outcome, compared to their peers? If so, what action have you taken to address this issue?
- Are the pupils who have poor ECM outcomes also those pupils who have poor attendance, are persistent absentees, have challenging behaviour, or who have been excluded from school for fixed periods of time?
- How are pupils on free school meals (FSM), who have special educational needs (SEN), learning difficulties/disabilities (LDD), or who are looked after children (LAC), young carers, travellers, refugees and asylum seekers achieving in the ECM outcomes, compared to their peers?
- How are you working with external partners to remove barriers to learning resulting from pupils having poor emotional health and psychological well-being?
- How well is the school meeting its safeguarding responsibilities on safer recruitment of staff and the handling of any allegations of abuse?
- Is the standard of pupils' behaviour generally good? Is it getting better, worse or staying the same? What are the reasons for any decline in the behaviour of pupils, and what has the school done to address this?
- Are there any groups of pupils in the school who are not participating in school activities, community volunteering or having a 'voice'? If so, how will this be addressed?
- Do pupils understand their rights and responsibilities, and respect others who are different from themselves?
- Do some sections of the local community have negative perceptions of the behaviour of some children or young people who attend the school? If so, what are you doing to improve this situation and build more positive links with local residents?
- How effectively is the school working in partnership with other services to tackle particular issues affecting the well-being of pupils?
- Which pupils are engaging most frequently with extended services? How has this engagement had a positive impact on improving their well-being?

This list of questions is by no means definitive, but it does provide a good starter for drilling down to explore further the school's ECM outcomes.

1 How safe do you feel in school?

2 How well does the school do in tackling any bullying incidents?

3 Which adult(s) do you go to in school to talk to if something is worrying you?

4 How does the school encourage pupils to be healthy and lead a healthy lifestyle?

5 How are you helped to learn and make good progress at school?

6 If you need extra help or support with school work, who will provide this?

7 What is pupil behaviour like in school?

8 Are pupils treated fairly, equally and with respect by staff in school?

9 How well do school staff listen to pupils' views and act on them to make things better for pupils?

10 How does the school help pupils to understand and respect others from different cultures and backgrounds?

11 Are pupils able to do things for themselves and help others by raising money for charity, or by working on projects for the community?

12 How does the school help pupils to manage their own feelings and behaviour?

13 Does the school offer its pupils a good range of lunchtime and after-school clubs and activities?

14 Does the school help pupils to develop good life skills to prepare them for the future?

15 What is good about being a pupil at your school?

Figure 5.2 Pupil survey on the ECM outcomes

From: *Implementing the Every Child Matters Strategy*, Routledge © Rita Cheminais 2010

1 Do you consider your child enjoys being at school and is happy at school?

2 Do you feel that your child is making enough progress at school?

3 How do you know that your child enjoys their learning?

4 Do you consider your child is safe and well cared for when at school?

5 What does the school do to ensure your child develops good safety awareness?

6 Would you consider that the behaviour of pupils overall is good at the school?

7 Do you feel that the school treats your child fairly and with respect?

8 What does the school do to ensure that your child leads a healthy lifestyle?

9 What does the school do to help your child make a positive contribution within the school, and in the wider community?

10 Do you feel the school offers your child a good range of lunchtime and after-school clubs, activities, educational visits and trips?

11 How do you know that the school takes account of children's views?

12 Do you feel that the school prepares your child well for their move to the next year group, school, college, or for the future world of work?

13 Does the school make you and other parents feel welcome?

14 What does the school do to help parents to support their child's learning and well-being?

15 Do you feel the school listens to your views and those of other parents?

16 Do you consider that Every Child Matters in the school?

Figure 5.3 Parent survey on the ECM outcomes

1 What does the school do to promote the well-being of its pupils and staff?

2 How far are the views of staff, pupils and parents listened to and acted upon?

3 What does the school do to keep its pupils safe and well cared for?

4 How does the school ensure its pupils are healthy and lead healthy lifestyles?

5 What does the school do to ensure pupils enjoy their learning and achieve their optimum potential?

6 What does the school do to enable pupils to make a positive contribution?

7 What does the school do to enable pupils to achieve economic well-being?

8 How well does the school address pupils' emotional, social and behavioural difficulties?

9 Do you consider the school supports its staff well enough to enable them to promote pupils' ECM well-being?

10 Do you consider that Everyone matters within the school community?

Figure 5.4 Staff survey on the ECM outcomes

OFSTED surveys for key stakeholders on ECM

OFSTED will continue to utilise parent and pupil questionnaires/surveys as one method of seeking their views on aspects of the school's work. These also give inspectors an impression of pupils' and parents' satisfaction levels with the school, which can be tested out during inspection. These OFSTED questionnaires/surveys include questions relating to the five ECM outcomes and pupil well-being. These surveys, along with the staff survey, can be downloaded from the OFSTED website at www.ofsted.gov.uk.

Schools often undertake their own annual survey of pupils' and parents' views, which helps to provide additional supporting evidence for the SEF. Figure 5.2 offers a model school pupil survey, focused largely on gathering children's and young people's views in relation to the five ECM outcomes.

Figure 5.3 provides a model parent survey that school leaders may opt to utilise, in addition to the OFSTED parent questionnaire. This is focused once again on seeking the views of parents about the school's work in promoting pupils' well-being and the five ECM outcomes.

The OFSTED staff surveys, first introduced with the renewed inspection schedule in September 2009, are voluntary, and staff do not have to complete one if they do not wish to do so. Figure 5.4 offers an example of a staff survey.

Questions for further reflection

1 How are you targeting the improvement of particular aspects of the ECM outcomes?
2 In which ECM outcomes are gaps being narrowed and for which groups of pupils?
3 What is most effective in improving ECM outcomes in our school/setting and why?
4 What is the ECM pupil-level data telling you about outcomes? Are there any surprises?
5 How effective is the school/setting in addressing the ECM outcomes?
6 What does the school do to ensure there is good robust evidence for each of the five ECM outcomes to contribute to the SEF?
7 How detailed is the school's/setting's evaluation of ECM beyond the classroom?
8 What is the evidence gathered on the five ECM outcomes telling the senior leadership team about the impact of provision on pupils' well-being?
9 How does the school's/setting's performance in the ECM outcomes compare with that of other school's locally, and with the national average?
10 How far is the school publicly committed to helping to promote and contribute to improving children's and young people's ECM outcomes, that goes beyond the immediate school community?

Glossary

Children's Trust – is a local authority area partnership which brings together public, private, community and voluntary sector organisations responsible for services for children, young people and families to reduce inequalities, address poverty and improve future prospects.

Children's workforce – refers to all those practitioners and professionals from children's services such as health, social care and education, who work with children and young people in a range of education settings.

Commissioning – refers to the process of assessing local needs, planning and designing appropriate services to meet identified needs; monitoring and assessing the effectiveness and impact of the services provided.

Distributed leadership – refers to the distribution and delegation of aspects of leadership across different staff at all levels in order to divide tasks and responsibilities up more equitably.

Every Child Matters – is a government initiative designed to address the well-being needs of the whole child in relation to ensuring that all children and young people are healthy, safe, enjoy and achieve, make a positive contribution and achieve economic well-being.

Every Child Matters Standards – provides a self-evaluation framework of 12 standards, each aligned to the five Every Child Matters outcomes, which support the gathering of evidence in enabling a range of education settings to work towards achieving the national Every Child Matters Standards Award.

Leading teacher – refers to those teachers who are on the upper pay spine within a school, with a teaching and learning responsibility point in respect of the good and outstanding work they undertake.

Looked after child – refers to any child in the care of the local authority, or who is provided with accommodation by the local social services department for a continuous period of more than 24 hours.

Multi-agency working – is where those from more than one agency/service work together jointly, sharing aims, information, tasks and responsibilities.

National Service Framework – provides a set of quality standards for health, social care and some education services, aimed at reducing inequalities in service provision.

Partnership – refers to a group of professionals from different services/agencies joining together to collectively take responsibility for intervening early in order to remove barriers to learning and improve pupil well-being.

Personalisation – refers to service users being actively engaged in shaping and informing the development and delivery of appropriate services to meet their needs.

Personalised learning – embraces every aspect of school life, and is the process of tailoring and matching teaching and learning around the way different pupils learn in order to meet their individual needs, interests and aptitudes.

Provision map – provides an at-a-glance overview of the range of additional and different provision to address a diversity of pupils' learning and well-being needs.

School Improvement Partner – provides professional challenge and support to leaders in schools and pupil referral units in order to help them evaluate their school's performance, identify appropriate priorities for improvement and plan for effective change.

School improvement planning framework – introduced by the Training and Development Agency for Schools in 2008, the framework supports school leaders in aligning raising standards with pupil well-being.

School-level indicators – for pupil well-being are designed to evaluate and measure a school's contribution to promoting pupil well-being in respect of the five Every Child Matters outcomes. They are based on quantitative and qualitative information.

School report card – provides an at-a-glance overview of a school's standards and achievements, including performance against the five Every Child Matters outcomes.

Self-evaluation – refers to the process of gathering robust evidence on the day-to-day work of the school, which provides an honest assessment of its strengths and weaknesses.

Self-evaluation form – summarises evidence of the school's work in readiness for an OFSTED inspection, and is updated annually, forming only one part of a whole-school self-evaluation process.

Spiritual, moral, social and cultural development – is concerned with preparing children and young people for growing up into responsible, purposeful and sensible citizens who value and respect diversity in society. It also refers to their attitudes, morals and behaviour in society, developing their cultural understanding and interpersonal skills.

Strategic – refers to knowing what to achieve, justifying the direction taken and finding the best ways to get there.

Well-being – refers to having the basic things required to enjoy a healthy, safe and happy life. It also refers to the five Every Child Matters outcomes: be healthy; stay safe; enjoy and achieve; make a positive contribution; and achieve economic well-being.

Useful Websites and Resources

www.dcsf.gov.uk/everychildmatters
This website is the official government website and contains hundreds of guidance documents relating to implementing the Every Child Matters agenda.

www.ecm-solutions.org.uk
This website provides useful information about two national awards for children's centres, schools, academies and pupil referral units: the Every Child Matters Standards Award and the Multi-Agency Partnership Award.

www.nationalcollege.org.uk/ecmleadershipdirect
This website provides a bank of online resources to support school leaders and ECM managers in implementing Every Child Matters strategically.

http://onechildrensworkforce.cwdcouncil.org.uk
This website provides online access to the One Children's Workforce Framework for Children's Trusts, which supports the professional development of the wider children's workforce, who will be working in a range of educational settings such as children's centres and schools.

www.qcda.gov.uk/15949.aspx
This website enables you to download the useful QCDA publication, *Every Child Matters at the Heart of the Curriculum*, which exemplifies what the five Every Child Matters outcomes look like across all the subjects of the curriculum.

www.tda.gov.uk/remodelling/extendedschools/sipf2.aspx
This website provides access to the Training and Development Agency for Schools' *School Improvement Planning Framework* and the accompanying resources, some of which focus on Every Child Matters in the section of the framework entitled *Beyond the classroom*.

www.tda.gov.uk/about/publicationslisting/tda0672.aspx
This website provides access to the TDA publications page, where the ECM Manager can order the TDA/NCSL resource pack entitled *Engaging schools in sustainable Every Child Matters and extended services*.

www.teachers.tv/video/32325
This Teachers TV video, *Need to Know – Children's Trust*, offers a guide to the workings of Children's Trusts.

www.teachers.tv/search?q=School+Matters+Every+Child+Matters&t=1072%2C811
This page on the Teachers TV website has a good range of videos which focus on the Every Child Matters agenda, and aspects related to the five Every Child Matters outcomes.

References and Further Reading

Atkinson, M., Lamont, E., Murfield, J. and Wilkin, A. (2008) *Six Key Messages about ECM Leadership.* Slough: National Foundation for Educational Research.

Audit Commission (2008) *Every Child Matters: Are We There Yet?* London: Audit Commission.

CfBT/East Sussex County Council (2008) *Every Child Matters Quality Assurance ECM Outcomes Review Tool.* Sussex: Centre for British Teachers and East Sussex School Improvement Service.

DCSF (2007) *Contribution of Schools to Every Child Matters Outcomes: Evidence to Support Education Productivity Measures.* Nottingham: Department for Children, Schools and Families.

DCSF (2008a) *Schools' Role in Promoting Pupil Well-Being. Draft Guidance for Consultation.* Nottingham: Department for Children, Schools and Families.

DCSF (2008b) *21st Century Schools: A World-class Education for Every Child.* Nottingham: Department for Children, Schools and Families.

DCSF (2008c) *Evaluating Every Child Matters: The SIP's Role in Engaging the School.* Nottingham: Department for Children, Schools and Families.

DCSF (2008d) *2020 Children and Young People's Workforce Strategy: Report of the Children's Workforce Practitioners Workshops. A report for the 2020 Children and Young People's Workforce Strategy prepared by Policy Research Institute, Leeds Metropolitan University on behalf of CWDC.* Nottingham: Department for Children, Schools and Families.

DCSF (2008e) *What is a Children's Trust?* Nottingham: Department for Children, Schools and Families.

DCSF (2008f) *Children's Trusts: Statutory Guidance on Inter-agency Cooperation to Improve Well-being of Children, Young People and Their Families.* Nottingham: Department for Children, Schools and Families.

DCSF (2008g) *A School Report Card: Consultation Document.* Nottingham: Department for Children, Schools and Families.

Derbyshire County Council (2006) *Derbyshire Framework for Evaluating Every Child Matters Outcomes in and around Schools. How Well are We Doing Now? Guidance Notes: For Nursery, Infant, Junior, Primary, Secondary and Special Schools and Support Centres.* Matlock: Derbyshire Advisory and Inspection Service.

Ereaut, G. and Whiting, R. (2008) *What do We Mean by "Wellbeing"? And Why Might it Matter?* Nottingham: Linguistic Landscapes/Department for Children, Schools and Families.

Frederickson, N., Dunsmuir, S. and Baxter, J. (2009) *Measures of Children's Mental Health and Psychological Wellbeing: A Portfolio for Educational and Health Professionals. Introduction.* Swindon: GL Assessment.

GTC (2007) *Inter-professional Values Underpinning Work with Children and Young People. Joint Statement.* London: General Teaching Council for England.

GTC (2009) *DCSF/OFSTED: Indicators of a School's Contribution to Well-being Consultation. Consultation Response from the General Teaching Council for England.* London: General Teaching Council for England.

Kendall, S., Straw, S., Jones, M., Springate, I. and Grayson, H. (2008) *Narrowing the Gap in Outcomes for Vulnerable Groups. A Review of the Research Evidence.* Slough: National Foundation for Educational Research.

LGA (2008) *Narrowing the Gap: First Report.* London: Local Government Association.

Mongon, D. (2009) *Indicators of a School's Contribution to Well-being. NCSL Events in Support of the Ofsted/DCSF Consultation. Summary Report.* Nottingham: National College for School Leadership.

Murphy, M. (2008) 'ECM and standards: The missing link', *Ldr magazine,* June 2008, pp. 25–8.

NCSL (2005) *Engaging Parents through Networks. Effective Partnerships with Parents (EPPa).* Nottingham: National College for School Leadership.

NCSL (2008a) *ECM Premium Project. School Leadership, Every Child Matters and School Standards. Identifying Links between ECM and Improvements in School Standards. Report Summary.* Nottingham: National College for School Leadership.

NCSL (2008b) *ECM Premium Project. School leadership, Every Child Matters and School Standards. Levers for Leaders and Learning: a Toolkit for Leadership Development in Extended Schools.* Nottingham: National College for School Leadership.

NCSL (2008c) *What are We Learning About: Leadership of Every Child Matters.* Nottingham: National College for School Leadership.

NCSL (2008d) *Every Child Matters (ECM) The Best of ECM Leadership Direct.* Nottingham: National College for School Leadership.

NCSL (2009a) *Every Child Matters Prospectus.* Nottingham: National College for School Leadership.

NCSL (2009b) *Advocating Every Child Matters.* Nottingham: National College for School Leadership.

NCSL/TDA (2009c) *Engaging Schools in Sustainable Every Child Matters and Extended Services.* Nottingham: National College for School Leadership.

OFSTED (2008a) *TellUs3 National Report.* London: Office for Standards in Education, Children's Services and Skills.

OFSTED (2008b) *Indicators of a School's Contribution to Well-being. Consultation Document.* London: Office for Standards in Education, Children's Services and Skills.

OFSTED (2008c) *The Deployment, Training and Development of the Wider School Workforce.* London: Office for Standards in Education, Children's Services and Skills.

OFSTED (2009a) *Ofsted's Evaluation of the Autumn Term 2008 Pilot Inspections of Maintained Schools.* London: Office for Standards in Education, Children's Services and Skills.

OFSTED (2009b) *Ofsted's Evaluation Schedule of Judgements for Schools Inspected under Section 5 of the Education Act 2005, from September 2009.* London: Office for Standards in Education, Children's Services and Skills.

OFSTED (2009c) *Framework for the Inspection of Maintained Schools in England from September 2009.* London: Office for Standards in Education, Children's Services and Skills.

OFSTED (2009d) *Self-Evaluation Form.* London: Office for Standards in Education, Children's Services and Skills.

OFSTED (2009e) *Indicators of a School's Contribution to Well-being. An Evaluation Report: Responses to the Joint Department for Schools, Children and Families/Ofsted Consultation on Proposed Changes to Maintained School Inspections.* London: Office for Standards in Education, Children's Services and Skills.

QCA (2008) *Every Child Matters at the Heart of the Curriculum.* London: Qualifications and Curriculum Authority.

TDA (2007a) *Professional Standards for Teachers. Why Sit Still in your Career?* London: Training and Development Agency for Schools.

TDA (2007b) *Guidance on the National Occupational Standards for Supporting Teaching and Learning in Schools. Overview of Policy and Initiatives.* London: Training and Development Agency for Schools.

TDA (2008) *School Improvement Planning Framework.* London: Training and Development Agency for Schools.

West Midlands Regional Partnership (2008) *The Outcomes Framework. West Midlands Children's Commissioning Partnership (A working group of the West Midlands Regional Partnership).* Coventry: West Midlands Regional Partnership.

Index